Dedication

I dedicate this book to all who are lost and found. To those who are suffering and are healing. To everyone who has yearned for ground beneath their feet and something or someone to believe in. I hope this book brings you clarity. I hope it makes you thirst in all the right ways. I hope it brings you to God, or closer to him. I hope it helps you. Not everyone finds faith in the same ways. Some are born into a faithful family, some aren't exposed to religion at all, or are exposed to false idols. I found my faith by losing it when I never really had it to begin with. I found my faith when I was at my lowest, my weakest and most fearful. I found my faith when I lost myself and parts of me broke away that I wasn't supposed to get back. I found God through a small separation, a small death; that of my own. I found him and he set me new, he removed my heart of stone and gave me one of flesh. He restored me. He covered me. Sent his angels to guide me. He protected me, and loves me the way I love him.

    The most sacred part of my story; don't carry my death with you, but carry my message because it's worth more. Because he brought me back to life. God doesn't forsake us, he prepares us to be loved by him the son, prepares us to be worthy of the grace and glory of the holy spirit and be prepared for the everlasting kingship of God the father so we may work through and by faith towards our salvation. To be saved by our own hand instead of blotted out by it.

    To make us dead to sin, and alive to God.

Truly I ask of you, all who will read this book,

    Who is assigned to us that we can help save?

The mystery that can permeate through scars and wounds as divine timing peaks behind the curtain of revelations. We are the army of God and our words can be weaponized like swords not to maim, but to unbreak chains and bring forth sanctified grace to revive more of his image and likeness back. By light piercing through the dark to plant seeds of holiness and to tend among those who have endured vocational suffering. For us to all be granted wings alike angels, might like lions, and the purity of the lamb. To inspire truth, shed perversion and be united in the assembly to stand in line and pledge our blemished but whole souls before our creator. Not to lay down our amassed armor before him, but to lay down our weaknesses that stippled our footing toward sin and away from his face. To right ourselves by having done right by him. To see him so we can be seen with unadulterated righteousness and mercy.

    Who is assigned to us that we can save,
    so that we may also save ourselves?

This story will take you on my path and the brokenness that led me breaking to heal, going back in time to find that little girl I had been before she loved God, and saving her to save my soul in becoming the woman I am today.

Yours, Deanna Marie Battista

"Holiness is not for wimps and the cross is not negotiable sweetheart, it's a requirement."

Mother Angelica

Table of Contents

Forward ix

Introduction 1

Chapter One • In the Beginning 5

Chapter Two • Consequence of Love Is Pain 11

Chapter Three • The Boy in the Royal Blue Sweatshirt 27

Chapter Four • The Allure of Healing Painlessly 47

Chapter Five • Death of Me 55

Chapter Six • Consequence of Pain 57

Chapter Seven • The Undoing That Was Choosing Good or Evil ... 61

Chapter Eight • Rendition of Responsibility 67

Chapter Nine • Breaking to Heal 71

Chapter Ten • The Releasing of a Dove 81

Chapter Eleven • Falling to Grace 83

Chapter Twelve • The Resurrection of Me 85

Chapter Thirteen • To Venerate My Soul 91

Chapter Fourteen • God Showed Me His Heart and Ignited Mine ... 95

Chapter Fifteen • The End Is Just the Start 103

Outro 107

Final Word 109

In Loving Memory 111

About The Author 112

"God is my Father and Heaven is my Mother."
St. Philomena

Forward

I haven't been broken to pieces like I always thought I had; I've been broken to peace.

1 Samuel 16:7

"But the Lord said to Samuel, 'Do not look on his appearance or on the height of his stature, because I have rejected him; for the Lord does not see as mortals see; they look on the outward appearance, but the Lord looks on the heart.'"

Introduction

My name is Deanna Marie, and I would like to introduce myself to the beautiful soul that picked up this book. This has been a long time in the making; me being a published writer that is. I would first like to talk about my beginning and how my life experiences and personal loss brought me to creating this resuscitation of the ground beneath my feet, the breath in my lungs, and the beating within my heart that is scribed with faith beyond sight of God's love.

    I was raised by three parents; my grandparents Papa and Nonna, and my amazing Mom. When I was two years old I was diagnosed with Juvenile Rheumatoid Arthritis. I had been sick for a long time before that, and after countless tests, doctor's appointments and hospital visits, my symptoms finally showed enough to get an official and proper diagnosis. I have been in and out of the hospital from a very young age, fear continuously being instilled within me. Nursing this anxiety and fear became adjacent to my childhood and this led to many hurdles throughout the years. I've been medicated with countless prescribed drugs and injections since the age of two. My Mom very quickly had to learn how to become not just a single mother but a nurse, an advocate, a therapist, a voice of comfort and a defender for me. My Mom fought for me since the day she found out she was pregnant. From the very start of my beginning there were people and circumstances that advised her not to bring me into this world. She did not waiver, she did not bend or let fear, or anyone come between her as the mother she already had become and the child (daughter) she would give birth to who she knew would be "as bright as day." Me, Deanna Marie!

My Mom fought for me before she knew me, and this is the first example I would like to highlight of the glory of God within my life. God fights for us, his children and loves us unwaveringly. Nothing and no one could ever deconstruct the love God has for mankind. Every man and woman, every child in and out of the womb. He loves us as only a Father could. My Mom fought for me, and on November 27th, 1999 - twenty-four years ago I was born. Thank you Mom for safeguarding me. Mostly, thank you for your endless fight in being my Mother always.

As a young child I was often isolated and alone when I was sick and stuck in bed, countless procedures and joint injections to remove the inflammation. Jra is a double edged sword; the autoimmune disorder that comes with this chronic illness always made me not feel well. From kids in school picking on or ignoring me, to teachers dehumanizing, ostracizing and belittling me. To doctors and nurses hurting me for the sake of helping me, or just hurting me. I was riddled with fear and illness for years. I would like to highlight something about my illness later on in this book, something wonderful, until then…

    Aside from my illness, and the hardships that this led my childhood to carry, I want to detail every single brick that laid my foundation to the creation of this book. I will take you on a journey through loss, losing loved ones, losing myself, dealing with severe anxiety, seeking out God in the wrong places, worldly vices and confusion. As well as my story of coming to grace and eventually finding Jesus, the most important piece to the puzzle of putting my trust back together, my broken spirit, my broken and contrite heart.

Romans 8:26

"The spirit helps us in our weakness; for we do not know how to pray as we ought, but that very spirit intercedes with sighs too deep for words."

Chapter One
In the Beginning

My first experience with death that I can remember, was almost of my own. I was six years old and caught an infection. Mom and I had to go to different hospitals. Test after test and countless days and weeks spent finally settled at Albany Medical Center and I started to mend. But before that I remember several things; first my diagnosis was determined to be a Staph infection vs Jra. I was in the hospital for three weeks. The doctor told my Mom if the infection went to my heart or brain I wouldn't have survived. I remember being weak, scared and helpless. But I also can recall not as much the healing part, but the fighting part. I was sick for so long then one day I wasn't. Just like that. Maybe that's how it seemed to me, being so little. I know for my Mom it felt like time had stopped. The doctors treated me, and gave me medication to help me; eventually I got better. It might not have been as quick as I remember it, but in an instant life and death can be so close yet so far apart, and so can war.

My body fought a ruthless war inside of me, I never knew this war would continue but the translation would be different later on in my life. At this age the "enemy" if you will, was the infection in my body. Years after; I would mend and get better, then sick and better and sick and better. Again and again this vicious repetitive cycle felt never ending. Being sick and being healed are two things I thought I knew very well. I did, to an extent. There are many infectious diseases known in the medical field. However there are new kinds of infections of old (known by professionals of a different sort, those within the Catholic church) that took hold of my endless vulnerable state. The infection of sin to mankind is a part of history and the history of the creation of the paradise we reside in. For like many, due to my innocence and naiveness, I fell into the category of mankind who did not know of sin. It is and has been unbeknownst to many, we truly can become our worst enemy because by our own hand we oftentimes desecrate the image of God or the honor of which we don't carry ourselves with, that we are meant to as children of his. For examples not of my own accord, but so my audience may understand intrinsically. Such as plummeting into things like vanity that bleeds into self-hate, and even potentially self-harm. Promiscuous behavior in the name of empowerment that bleeds into self-doubt and a question of self-worth and self-esteem. Again, not experiences I have faced of my own account, but ones that I have bared witness too. Note how many times the word "self" resurfaces. We were made in the image of God, but then sin entered into paradise and original sin took root. There was a separation of a self from Adam and Eve. The death of our spirit. This is why we have to get baptized to resuscitate ourselves with and restore grace to the soul, like the breath of life God gave to Adam that he then lost once after he ate of the fruit God had warned him against. There were many separations and deaths that followed. As so begins this internal battle and war that many people go their whole life without realizing, and also without the one tool to survive it all; God.

    The purpose of being created in an image, is to reflect that image. Once original sin entered we were made like the image of Adam. Until more of God's mercy and love for us took root in our world and his covenant with Noah held true. That being said, we have to have more than just faith in God. We have to work towards our salvation, and our reunion with the spirit and soul connected like God had always intended. We have to be purified, and cleansed and " lead not into temptation" and have God to "deliver us from evil." Sin got in and still God chose to create a covenant with Noah after he removed all the wickedness of humankind by the great flood.

    This can prefigure the storm and great flood that can happen within all of ourselves, and even more so than the damage this creates, but the inability to let out a dove from inside our hearts when you try to do so without him.

So, when it came to me personally finding my footing within this world, this was my experience. I was born and raised in an Italian and Catholic family. We didn't pray everyday, or go to church every Sunday. Around the holidays we would go to church or for a special occasion in the family, a wedding, a baptism, first communion, or losing a loved one. So I didn't have a clear and concise understanding of faith. I had an understanding of always being sick, missing school and being nervous to go back because of the way teacher's would treat me. I had a profound understanding of hard working parents. Papa and Nonna; always working hard towards the American dream after becoming citizens in this country to create a family to share it with. My Mom working endlessly to keep me healthy and happy in spite of when I was sick; was an understated full time job. Juggling my health while ignoring her own. Doctors offices and hospitals were where she was the most with me if not right by my bedside at home, or at the dining room table teaching me and helping me with my homework and reading so I wouldn't fall behind. These were the pillars of amazing, self-less, compassionate parents who raised me. I was raised by three parents instead of one, or two. My young life revolved around family, and health and Papa holding me so Mommy could give me shots to make me feel better. They all became my home and my safety. Yet I never knew one of the most important pillars someone could have was severely missing. God. I had some understanding of my Catholic faith, just not much. Mommy read to me and bought me a bible, I was baptized as a baby and had my first communion. I attended Sunday school classes up until I was in the fourth grade because of the Jra my Mom had no choice but to keep me home and discontinue my religious education. I had not received my confirmation at that point but also didn't realize what I was losing out on. I want to preface by saying my "faith" then, which didn't really resemble any, was how my Mom was taught with her's and Nonna with her's as well. No one was to blame for my knowing of God, but not knowing him. I actually think my coming to grace happened just the way it was meant to. Read this bible verse I will share with you of many that resonated with me in my faith journey; Psalm 51:17 - "The sacrifice acceptable to God is a broken spirit, a broken and contrite heart."

In order for me to know my creator in heaven, I had to go through many trials, and much suffering, some of which was of my own choice's I had not realized then.

Mark 8:35

*"For those who want to save their life will lose it,
and those who lose their life for my sake,
and for the sake of the gospel, will save it."*

Chapter Two
Consequence of Love Is Pain

My next experience with death was the worst that could have rang out and is how it became the undoing of me, which is what saved me in the end and brought me here today. Prior to this shattering experience, let me first explain who Papa was to me and how we both were led to that hospital room on December the 19th of 2013. Let me explain how all of this transpired within the same place I had fought for my life countless times over before from being ill and in between the lull of waiting to be sick again. Where I would again have to face and fight through the symphony of pain and brokenness that evil would then toy with. Especially for the last delicate parts of me Papa's last breath had left me with.

    Growing up I mentioned before, I had three parents instead of two or what would have been only one. So thus began Papa filling the shoes of what would have been my Father's, so much so that he made new ones. Creating the foundation and rock solid ground of what a man, father, and a lionheart looked like. He depleted away worry, and what would have been more pain and suffering not having my biological "Dad" in my life. Papa made it so no tears needed to be wiped away from my heart. Papa bear always did things his way, and this wasn't any different; he made it so there wasn't ever a thought of what was missing, because nothing ever was. The factors that led to my Father not being in my life were of his own struggles and demons to battle with that no one deserves. The price paid for that kind of admission around sin is a sting that doesn't ever go away. Yet my Mother and I ultimately paid a different price because of this. With the grace and determination that Papa had for us, that price wasn't much. Nothing like it could have been. Actually it was more of a gift and that hurts me a little to admit. The fruit that grew within and around my childhood even while dealing with my health so severely. Papa was always there to keep me smiling anyway. He kept my will strong, and he always held me through the worst of it all. Always being in his arms during the agony of the fear and the pain my little body had to endure. Especially when my Mom would have to give me injections to help slow the progression of the disease. He was always there without fail, they all were. But Papa became the glue, the hand I'd reach for, and the one to wipe my tears away with laughter. He felt immense pain in his heart in holding me the way he did to help Mom and I. To see me in pain was one thing, but to hold me in pain was another.

To even think you can get used to seeing your child sick is daunting. I can't even imagine what it must have been like on their end. Papa, Nonna's and Mom's. He would cry with me sometimes, always trying his best to hide it. It grieved him terribly, my suffering and it eventually became his own, just like my Mother's. They learned to suffer with me. Yet he never faltered, not just from his responsibility, but always going the extra mile to be more than just present. He made sure he was wrapped around my heart completely as I was his. He was my cloud in the fourteen years I had him in my life, and I was always his angel. Now the roles are reversed.

But within those fourteen years, he not only raised me, nurtured and provided for me. He loved me fiercely, helped my Mom heal me as much as he humanely could. He taught me how to measure and give kindness back to others even when they "didn't" deserve it. He was the prominent example of what a king looked like. The man who always took care of his girls, and of his family. The lengths to which he would go to uplift my pain and work around it rather than just trying to make it go away when even the doctors couldn't. Everytime I would have to travel to doctors for surgeries (joint aspirations) at Shriners Hospital; Papa would always rent a limo for my Mom and I to drive in just to make the daunting reality that always laid before me wrapped in a sphere of torment somewhat better. He always made everything better, even when he was dying. It was hard to see then, the amazing things he would do for me. It was not only hard for me because I was young, but mostly when my pain stained tears always blurred my vision. Underappreciative is the catalyst that can be applied to everyone around Papa, including me. He was always there for me, until he wasn't.

So every story goes, happiness can only last so long until it stops. Until death do we part, was the pinnacle of the despair I faced. The beautiful man I used to dream about walking me down the aisle one day to my prince charming. It wasn't just the notion of him being sick. It wasn't even the word cancer. It was the question mark that hung in the balance over our heads, but no more than it did Papa's. But there was no way he wasn't going to get better right? Wrong. This was the word my Mom told me one day after school. "This is so wrong, but it's what's going on and I have to tell you Papa has cancer." I cried, though I didn't know why because I didn't know what the forbidden word meant. I just knew that it was bad. So I cried and wondered until Mom and I drove to the barber shop to get him that evening. I walked in and there Papa was, the very next day after his diagnosis; at work cutting a customer's hair. I walked in and just stopped to look at him. It was in his eyes, the hurt. They reflected mine. I went to sit down not knowing what to do or say. I became quiet. I felt this darkness close to me I had never felt before that wasn't from me being sick. I never felt it around me when I was in the in between; the before me getting sick again. Once the customer left, the air and the room itself became harsh and too close. Papa's wellbeing wasn't alright even though things seemed "normal." Though this day it was harder for him to smile I remember. Papa was always the pillar of strength, because that was where I'd always get mine from. To see him not quite himself because of this one word, I didn't know what to do to make him better. At the age of thirteen this confused me because yes the word cancer is bad, maybe even really bad, I thought. But I didn't take it for the death sentence it was. I don't think any of us did until it was too late, Papa especially. So when Papa saw that his face wasn't the only one missing a smile, he put on his blue suede jacket and walked outside. A few minutes passed and Mom started cleaning the shop like usual. I waited sitting there, staring at the door wondering if there was a chance it would never open again somehow. Then after a little time longer Papa walked back in a little pep in his step and handed me a vanilla milkshake from Stewart's. I smiled at him and his eyes were what smiled back at me. I remember many people telling me from that day on that my smile was Papa's favorite thing to see. It made him sad, not too. This day changed everything.

So three or four weeks after the stage 4 diagnosis of carcinoma cancer that spread to his lungs and everywhere else was all we had been left with. Even with a second opinion to plan; what we thought would be his recovery. No, not his recovery but his death. This, I did not understand. The longest I had gone without Papa being there were times I was stuck in the hospital. This time was different though, because it was him that was sick and I wasn't. I didn't know how to wrap my mind around the fact that I wasn't the patient but that Papa-bear was. That I was strong and he was becoming weak. I didn't know what to do with this information other than sit with it like it took form and became this thing that would sit next to me and follow me around. The longest I went without seeing or talking to Papa was a little over a week. He went to Arizona for a second opinion to see other doctors that were supposed to tell us he would be alright. That is the furthest from what happened. Instead, any hope was decimated and he had to have surgery to help him breathe from the tumors that were leaking fluid in his lungs. He was also put on an oxygen tank. This being said, I dreamt in my head what it would be like when he came back home. He would jump out of the car and I would run to him like I always had as a little girl. I would jump into his arms and give him the biggest hug that would cure the cancer away since the doctors couldn't. When the car pulled into the driveway though, this was not what happened. My excitement and anticipation wore out when the doors wouldn't open fast enough. So there I ran down the steps from the house and ran towards the driveway to the side of the car where I saw through the windshield those sunglasses he always wore even when he was indoors. I got to the car door and opened it with all the love and feeling I had missing him so much. The reality that struck me across my face and my spirit when I did though, it killed a little part of me. I felt it. The second time this happened where I felt myself lose a part of me in some way, I hadn't noticed it before until it was gone. I couldn't decipher exactly what it was that was now missing. But the departure of those little pieces felt like the decay of my heart since finding out he had cancer. Since that day when my Mom told me and the grace of which Papa handled and carried this news, not of the diagnosis itself but the news of me now knowing too, it was astonishing. Almost to the point where that hurt more. That was him though, worried about those around him instead of himself or the worry about tomorrow. Only the present. Only today. That was his superpower. His courageous resolve about the way he genuinely cared for others, over himself and more times than just in the end, over his own health. So seeing him for the first time after over a week without, was the longest I had ever been away from him. It was heart wrenching. How sick he had gotten in such a short amount of time. How much weight he had lost, the color in his face drained, the sparkle that was in his eyes now gone. Even more so, his personality had lessened along with his very being. Seeing him not be him, it tore me apart but not more so than my hesitation when I saw him looking back at me; Papa seeing me taking him in. The unruliness and mercilessness of his condition. I think it tore him apart more. I think I broke his heart after the reality that we could no longer ignore broke mine. I was so careful and slow in the hug I gave him. Ignoring my fear, ignoring his appearance, the solemn despair in the air and how quiet and sad everyone was around us. I tried in that moment to hold him like he always had me. I never knew to be delicate with Papa-bear. The moment I realized I had more life in me than he did, I felt like whatever would happen, I wanted it to be with me alongside him.

He hadn't gotten to start chemo and the hospital was where we would inevitably end up; from that last day we spent together in the new place we were going to call home but never did. This felt like a searing start of something that everyone seemed to know but me. I held his hand as he lay in bed with the daunting understanding and pain that he was dying, surrounded by all who loved and hurt him. It's amazing what little things matter that used to so much, when it's life and death that teeter's on the clock's hand calling out someone's name. Forgiveness is something Papa knew very well. Too well for my liking, honestly. But can one know it too well? I think my perception of this was faulty. One can have many things they overcome in this life, but without the ability to forgive once is deafening to oneself, but the ability to forgive seventy seven times over. That's in comparison to the likeness and image in which God created us. 'Kill them with kindness' was Papa's infamous line for any and all situations that would occur. It's not about the word kill, it's about the brunt force in which you still choose over and over to love, give love and not take away love for those that have wronged you. Though this was all before I knew Jesus well enough to know where such inspiration could come from. Papa knew. Parts of him within forgiveness were really a reflection of him in his ability to hold not just the tenderness for others but mercy measured illimitably and give it to everyone back tenfold. I only hope to be a fraction of warmhearted as them both.

    I had never been presented with life and death so closely together before. Never seeing death actually take shape in this world. Not even the notion of departure can sound loud enough since we are all so desensitized to "bad news" or "terrible things that can happen." I never held it in my hands before, just in my little body. There is a supposed difference I learned, and by my heavenly father the lesson that was about to impart within every part of me, would I. I had gone to many funerals and wakes with both Papa and Nonna over the years. Losing family members here and there, since I was so little I only remember so much. I remember Papa and Nonna both losing their sisters a few years apart from each other. I only ever saw the aftermath however. I never saw the destruction of it. I hadn't yet been pierced by death at this point. The silence that it really is, at least that was my experience. Once that last time home, before the paramedics brought Papa into the ambulance on a stretcher; Papa grieved in front of us and told us he wasn't going to come back home and that he was going to die. He told us, all of us. I was sitting right next to him when he did. Yet I heard but couldn't comprehend the finality of what he was saying. What that meant, he was going to die? What would that look like and what would happen afterwards? Questions and loss filled me and I felt wrong. I didn't have any tears to cry in those moments. I held his hand in both of mine thinking that would be enough to keep him here. Not in the new place we hadn't got to start calling home yet, but just with me. To stay close, I held on as delicately tight as I could. I felt his tears like pangs of rain on the windowpane of my heart. But still I didn't believe it. I saw with my eyes and heard with my ears. I even felt the weight around my heart. But my mind told me otherwise. Still I chalked it up to "everything will be okay" because that is what he always told me, and he was always right. I would get better. Almost like I needed to hear him tell me that so I could. In the hospital, we were there for a few days. I never wanted to leave him, especially at night. Not just for the sake of him not being alone. But the point of me not wanting to leave the foot of his bed, just in case. In case "something bad" happened. In case something good; in case he got better and we could go back to Stewart's, get scratch off tickets, play the lotto and get cotton candy ice cream. It didn't ring out to be the velocity of sound, what was really happening. But the silence all the truth held that I didn't eventually would shatter. It felt like I was losing puzzle pieces of me, Papa and my childhood with him in just the few days we were at the hospital. It's almost as if everytime I had to leave him at night, I was leaving parts of myself too that weren't there for me to recognize the next morning I'd see him again. The less I'd recognize him, the more I'd fail to recognize my reflection too. So every morning though the few that were, I would get up bright and early thinking that was how the day was going to go. But it didn't take long, I soon felt like time was our enemy and the hospital and doctors weren't doing anything but waiting. But what were they, and everyone else waiting for? He was talking and somewhat smiling and then he stopped, he was drinking and eating until he didn't want to anymore. He would walk around until we started to wheel him around in a wheelchair. I think we only got to do this once or twice. "Hi stranger" Papa would always say to me after a bout of sickness and I just started to get my energy back enough to sit at the dinner table and eat a little. The sunlight was shining all around him and me, "hi stranger" I said looking at him. Everyone around the room looked solemn. He tried his best to smile but didn't, couldn't. I remember looking at the ground uncertainty rattling all around me. He really did look like a stranger now, my heart sank and I worried if I had hurt his feelings. The warm sunlight enveloped me like a hug from heaven that I didn't think twice about. It looked as if my words had hurt him somehow. Not the phrase itself but every memory behind them I think. Time used to be my friend when I was okay. But I know all too well how time can quickly become your adversary when you aren't. This too I would learn in the darkest of ways.

    Once back in his hospital room, that is where he would stay. Hours seemed to turn into days and yet minutes seemed to turn into seconds. I tried to stay close by staying away. I didn't know this feeling, this emotion, this fear if that's what it was. Afraid of even the fear lacing its tether around my memories but now it was pain they would bring me. This is something else that I couldn't understand. Why could Papa holding my hand and bringing me to the pet store now hurt me somehow? Why would this bring tears to my eyes? The dread I would feel everytime Mom would have to give me medicine and Papa would have to hold me, this I now longed for. Even with the fear and the suffering that would come with it. I just wanted him to hold me always. This odd feeling that maybe he wouldn't, started to trickle in every footstep I took away from his hospital room. I thought if I kept my distance, maybe that would make him feel better. The last thing I wanted was him to look at me with such sadness in his eyes. Be careful what you wish for is an understatement. The next time I would see Papa's face would be with his eyes closed and this is how they would stay until his heart stopped beating. I didn't realize this though. I just knew he needed rest to get better. That he was just sleeping, and we were all waiting for him to wake up soon. Not until after his eyes were closed did I stay closer after the posed question and phrase "hi stranger." It felt like he was so close but so far away. We stayed there in that room for hours that day, usually we always did but something about that last day seemed different. Less people were around, more people cared less to stay. Papa's brother was visiting and had stayed by his side throughout that time. He sat on the left of Papa where Nonna sat at the right side of him. My Mom sat in a chair close to me and across from Nonna. I stood leaning against the wall looking down at my feet, waiting. I always knew that was my place. At the foot of his bed, I'm not sure why but that is where my heart longed to be. Then it happened. I thought, the greatest thing that ever could. Everyone was talking and Papa, sleeping as he had been, moved. He moved his head a little, and the relief that floated through me was nothing like getting over all the times I had been sick put together. I stood firm looking at him. Waiting for his eyes to meet mine and I'd show him my smile that he of course would mirror. But that didn't happen either. Instead he moved his head a little then to the side as he took a deep long breath. Peaceful and slow, all within a few seconds and at the same time. When his head dropped more so after this, is when I called his name. That's when we all started to call out his name. I cried out to him somehow as the ground beneath my feet shifted all the energy grief can exude, awakening my fears and I screamed. I screamed and cried for him until time, the enemy that it had become; turned its horns towards me and blackness engulfed me. I don't remember how, but the next thing I can recall after my Mom and a nurse were holding me and trying to stop the never ending parade of my tears from drowning us all. Mom held me the way Papa wouldn't anymore. Sitting in a puddle of my tears and confusion my blurry vision began to register with me holding his hand that used to hold the sunshine within it. It felt different, cold and far away. But it was still him. The glass around my mind and understanding broke and I stayed there for hours until the doctors had to pull us all away. I felt like both my feet weighed one hundred pounds each. We stood motionless but our hearts beat, while Papa's wasn't anymore. Nothing could have prepared me for the sight that captured my vision. A stretcher was brought from his room as we waited in the hallway, again for what I had no idea. A bright red blanket covered something, someone. I peeked inside his room after my eyes finally let me look away. He wasn't there. Every part of me hurt. Every part of me mourned and cried with the realization I had just witnessed. They took him away before I got to say goodbye. Why would I have needed to say goodbye, the last thought before leaving the hospital as the moon's light paved the way through the darkness of my heart. He died. And I couldn't fathom that he no longer lived. I didn't want to either.

    That night through the loss, through the hurt and denial; darkness awaited my return. Time again looked as if it was mocking me through the absence of light. I sit in silence hearing the moon cry along with my heart. I turned and a door opened by itself. This accompanied with the feeling that came with it I would recognize… soon.

"In order to be fixed you have to be broken first"
-Deanna Marie

Chapter Three
The Boy in the Royal Blue Sweatshirt

Before Papa's passing everything seemed steady until it wasn't. Once everything started to break apart and away from what I knew, it didn't slow down or stop. It was like every peak of suffering and torment I faced, then unlocked a new level that I would have no choice but to endure. I felt the ground beneath my feet give way and there was nothing to hold onto. Let me take you back in time and explain the procession in which this happened without allowing me to catch my breath deep enough to sustain me without the notion that would cling to me with a vengeance; to break.

First we sold our house that had been in our family for over thirty years. It wasn't just the house my Mom had grown up in at one point. This was where my childhood was held. As I said, Papa knew forgiveness well. This was something I would have to learn myself immensely but over time. We moved due to circumstances that led to us living in another place Papa and Nonna curated and built out of love and permanence for their family. A beautiful place, though we weren't supposed to call it home. That being said, God works in mysterious ways especially through hardship. I wish I would have been able to see this then. I wish I would have been able to measure my heart the way Papa and Nonna did endlessly. Not just the capability in which they could love and give. Not in beats per minute either, but in their endurance for what could harm them so severely and still have it thrash inside their chests painfully or otherwise.

    I moved to another school the year prior and became the new girl. That part wasn't as bad as I had dreaded, but it was still harsh and the more that happened would then follow more change of everything I knew to be constant. Even around these painstaking moments right after one another in the span of only a year. Then eventually dwindled to only within the span of two months. It wasn't until the following year the worst of it all was going to happen aside from the impending doom my health always was. Almost like something aside from life was kicking me when I was already down. I can't even imagine how Papa must have felt. This I would soon be introduced to as the abstinence of life, death. So the fairytale world I had created in that backyard I had to leave behind and say goodbye to. I had to divulge into unforeseen territory around places and kids I didn't know. Changing schools, and even moving into the next town over was daunting but isn't what broke my heart. Aside from the dangling that was the unknown, it was losing my home that severed everything I held dear. Always being sick and having that one dreamscape my mind would make my home turn into. It was the safest place I'd ever known. Losing that felt like a variation of a sickness that hadn't healed because it couldn't. What medicine could make all that had happened until the next gut wrenching hit heal? Prior to his diagnosis, this was still the reality. We still had to move. But everything we had to leave behind, we didn't know what that would become. What was the cure? The decisions made by my parents were enacted as such, as a solution to such hemorrhaging problems. But as a young child, I didn't know this to be just that. A solution. It had been the only place I ever called home. But that wasn't what made it that. It was Papa, Nonna and Mommy who did. Then eventually a little beagle puppy I named Buddy Balboa. Papa got him for me two years earlier, just before my eleventh birthday. Everything was just "perfect." Any bad was what I had been used to, any sickness or hurt was what I had endured so many times before. I was used to surviving. I had found peace in moments of my life when there weren't many always being sick. Then the sickness brought on by being able to finally go to school would in turn make me ill from my teachers and the school faculty picking on me. It seemed to be constant. The reprieve of being better, to then catching that other kind of sickness I didn't know then most people refer to as anxiety. I didn't know then what dread and anxiety mixed together looked like. I only knew what it felt like. It wasn't enough to not feel well. It was even worse when I felt somewhat okay. I must have had some red x painted on me somewhere. The ruthless and mercilessness always made me feel faint even before the being talked down to would start again. Then the cycle would continue forever keeping me on my toes. I really felt like the bambina ballerina Papa used to call me. Any idea of me not feeling well and the wolves descend. After all that I went through, the only breath to aid in my bruises was coming home after a long day of being emotionally lashed. Home was my consolation. Whether it be from a battle at the hospital or coming back home from the battle that school became for me, ever since the first grade. This lasted until I started to notice my breath of relief didn't seem to be shared. To see Papa and Nonna stressed; it was a never ending question mark that only seemed to be on my mind. After every sickness, every recovery, every time after surgery. The relief in healing and the ability to say I'm okay and actually be, until the next cycle would return. It was amazing. But the relief I would feel after coming back home from war, I learned to hold my own hand when the wolves would come at me in packs of two or three. I thought one adult was plenty to issue hurt, let alone many. Whether it have been a teacher, school nurse, guidance counselor, lunch aid, or principal was bad enough. But to have to deal with multiple at once ganging up on me was a hellish experience that didn't seem to have any end. The only stop to this verbal pummeling was being so sick that it would make me go back to the hospital. Why didn't the comfort of being home and not having to endure the pain of my joints, or the fear in my tummy or the words that would be thrown at my feet and towards my little heart magnify enough for everyone to understand. Why didn't the three pillars of my heart talk about this feeling? This bliss. Moreso, why didn't they experience it with me when I did. Happiness and ease on their faces when I got better for the umpteenth time, of course. But why didn't that look on their faces stay? Sometimes mine wouldn't last either, but it always came back because of home. Why did the stresses of everyday life and around my family bore into this weight to carry that not even the warmth of home could remedy completely? How could I have not known this was God. Always with me, always near. Never dare too far away, even when I was. Why did the stress depart the breath I would finally be able to keep once all the bad went away. When did the grown up problems become so tenuous, I wondered watching for the years that led up to Papa getting sick. I always knew his sickness to be stress. I never knew it to be anything more or less. That house I felt was my time capsule and I wanted to keep it all. Not just the remembrance of the good and bad. I wanted to keep the good and bad itself. These roots of all my memories and the entirety of my childhood lay there in the morning glory flowers Nonna planted. In the cherub angel flower pots that lay in their place that even the cement knew belonged there. The funny umbrella tree that stood in all of its quirky delight, I didn't appreciate until I knew I would no longer see it everyday. The giant herkimer diamond boulder rocks I lugged back from a school field trip that lay way to Nonna's little circle flower forest that I swore was where fairies and unicorns lived. The shed where my little tiny hands would forever stay in dried foundation; which was exactly what I was losing. A part of the history of my heart. Where I first talked, walked, cried, and recovered. Not to mention all the Sunday family dinners. All my birthday parties, and the days where I couldn't move because it hurt too much. The pain and healing those walls held. The tears, the laughter, and everything Papa bear gave me. He was the heartbeat of that house and I became the soul. Mom fell into the lungs and Nonna the oxygen interlaced with the scent of lemon pledge and sauce with meatballs. Funny how many other vital organs there are and were missing (God). Having to say goodbye, it ruined a small part of me at first, this wound only grew over time. Some wounds time doesn't heal. I learned this too. But prior to the house selling and the fractures I began to experience I could only imagine hurt worse than breaking bones; I started high school.

    So now we continue back to the regularly scheduled program of my life imploding at the tender age of twelve. The fall from everything I once knew to be solid, everything around me including Papa turned to dust and the only everlasting I had after losing everything. A boy. Though this boy and I did not know each other, we weren't friends, we were strangers and unfortunate to say we never became friends either. He wasn't the prince I thought he might have been. Through no fault of his own or mine. At a young age this was terribly heart wrenching. But nonetheless, the impact this one person, one human being, one boy had on me. This was truly the start of everything. I think this was the road I was always meant to take. I was born suffering. This is what continued ruthlessly as the years went on .

The first day of high school came and went quickly, but the anticipation surrounding it was always that of excitement and color coordination thanks to my Mother. I picked out my outfit, my shoes, how I wanted my hair to look and everything that Mom and I always had to prep prior to the start of every new school year. Emails and doctors notes on board as well. She always had to expedite the process for any teacher to be informed of my illness and so they could understand. But no one ever understood. Not through my pain, not through my tears and not through my Mother's understandable anger. Though that will be detailed further, maybe in another story someday.

I walked to my first period class, study hall. Starting off my freshmen year with nerves, anxiety and intimidation of everyone who was taller and older than me. Even in my own grade I was always the youngest. So I walked, more like I ran to my class terrified I was late. Scared that the first day a teacher would already throw daggers for words in my direction. I was in such a hurry my schedule was upside down. I finally got to the doorway, I took a second to catch my breath or hold it. Something I was all too familiar with around school. But more than fear of my classmates, it was always what my teachers posed to only me that kept me afraid. I wait another second, and then I walk in expecting to see a room full of kids. To my surprise every seat was empty and there were chairs upside down on every desk. I stand in the doorway awkwardly trying to breathe normally while my lungs burn, and I clutch onto my class schedule for dear life. Then the color blue catches my eye. I turn and look up, across the room sitting alone looking at me is this brown-haired brown eyed boy wearing a royal blue sweatshirt. I smile at him, he smiles back waving his hand at me a little. We both say nothing. Not a hello, not one word. This is the story that changed everything for me. This is how our communication would continue for the next three years. We wouldn't say a word to each other. The boy in the royal blue sweatshirt became the cute boy I would see every now and again in the hallways. That same day my schedule changed so I no longer had a study hall with him. But the glimpses I would get made my heart flutter. My first real crush in high school, I'd like to think I was subtle about it. Of course I went home and told my Mom. What that boy meant to me the first day, was world's apart from what he would and still to this day means to me and symbolizes. God has such a mysterious way of wrapping his arms around us, his children and by the grace of these mysteries do we interact, talk, and are near those who can quite literally change our lives without realizing it. I should know. This boy changed mine.

Days and weeks went by and the boy in the royal blue sweatshirt was who'd I look for every time I opened the school doors or I heard the bell ring in between classes. I would look forward to seeing this cute brown haired boy with sweet eyes and a peculiar devotion to sneakers. I then would crush on the cute boy until the month of my birthday hit my world like a ton of bricks. It's astounding what a minute, a day, or even a month like November can deface. Three months of innocent puppy love, and then the world around me shattered. On November 2nd, 2013, Mom and I brought Papa to the emergency room for not feeling well and pains. This is where Papa had been diagnosed with stage four cancer. I fell asleep in the chair next to his hospital bed. Hours passed and tests were taken. The doctor on call pulled my Mom aside and told her first, then they explained everything to Papa. I didn't know until the very next day after school when Mom broke the news to me. Following this heartbreak, we all faced another one.

The house sold and we finally fully moved into the other house Papa and Nonna had built a few years prior. This was something that I carried heavily but not more than the idea of Papa being sick, still without realizing what it really meant. Then came another hit of pain and anguish that followed; oddly enough this had been heavier to bear than the first two initial blows. Papa had to sign over his barber shop for someone else to run since "he wasn't going to get better," which seemed to be the unspokeness that sounded around the air. He was sick was all I remember thinking to myself, how many times had I been, but had gotten better afterwards. To watch the slow burn of Papa losing what meant most to him. I can't put into words what that felt like to witness. It was as if I could reach out to touch the air around him and I would be able to feel his affliction. He cried in the car afterwards. He was forced to rip out his own heart out of his chest. He couldn't hide his pain, not even from me. He wasn't a prideful man, but it was my smile he cherished to keep alive more than anything else. When he couldn't it hurt us both. But this was different. This sight before me, my Mom talking him through it. I didn't know what or how to feel. I didn't know how to make it better. That was the part that weighed heavily on me the most.

 The day we moved in was on my thirteenth birthday. November 27th. The last birthday I would get to spend with Papa. I didn't know this then. He was wasting away so quickly and yet I still couldn't comprehend. Time like I mentioned was not my friend, even though I wasn't sick it felt worse than being sick or even in the hospital. It felt like another way to suffer I hadn't been introduced to before.

But with any introduction, they usually don't last. This one did. I didn't like it, the helplessness of it all. Papa had been too sick to sit at the table and sing. I remember how sad it made me. It was small, not anything like Mom usually did things. But she still made the effort despite all the grief that was all around us. It was impossible to ignore. I blew out my candles that year with tears wrapped around my wishes that I knew just wouldn't come true. I was almost angry, and that made me feel terrible. How could I be angry at the one person who's always been there. He was just so tired and couldn't sit up. Who was I to have my feelings hurt about what he couldn't even control, let alone expect him to be driven by my tender heart to be well enough. He didn't feel good. This is something that amassed heavy guilt in my innocent and delicate nature that was being irrupted by this world and all it had to offer. How would I have known inside the constructed bubble Mom, Papa, and Nonna had built just for me. Once construction was over, I tended to it myself over the years. I loved being in my bubble. Never going past the end of my driveway. Never leaving what I knew to be safe. Never leaving my parents. Of course at the age of twelve, now thirteen there wasn't much opportunity for that to occur. But it's something that I never yearned away from. Even now, I can't imagine not being with them. Nonetheless, I could have wished that day with that cake and those candles for him to get better, but I didn't. I thought it was hopeless. If only I would have known how to pray then. If only I would have known God. Then I guess I wouldn't be sitting here writing you all this story of how he showed me who he was so I could in turn show all of you. When the realization formed that years later I could have prayed for him but didn't, that was a whole other extent of remorse that I too carried. The word justice comes to mind. What is it about double edged swords that makes them so sharp to begin with? What is it about forgiveness that cuts through anything; even immorality? This too was what I would soon face.

But before I tear out my own heart writing that part of the story, let's get back to the sweetest part of this sadness. The beauty of what could have been in the mind of a thirteen year old whose world was crumbling all around her except just before the ground that cute boy walked towards but always away from. Me.

So once November hit, the punches never stopped, and neither did time. So Papa being sick and in and out of the hospital, gave me the reprieve and star I always wished on for me to hold. But the steel weight of it was a curse. He was sick and I wasn't. I went to school and barely missed any days until tragedy struck. So as the mornings bled into afternoons and the nights bled into puddles of tears and disillusion. Papa got worse and I got better. How this could be when I felt the suffering right alongside him, I don't know. Something kept my arthritis at bay. Whatever could it have been, or who? Like the distance the moon poses in the sky, so close but so far away, night came over my heart and he died. The time that rang around me felt like sheer excitement at the face of my grief. The excitement coming from the darkness for the girl they'd shadow for a time to come bellowed. How unforgiving they are to God's children. Is that what they carry themselves? Yet all the while still imploring the idea that they are better and know better than our creator. How broken the good can become, I know this all too well. The angels fell and what they became was not God's fault. It was a reflection of their disdain for anything that had to do with God's glory that wasn't their own. They blotted out their own light and shredded their wings to follow the devil. It's hard to even judge them. Who am I to, when I've done the exact same thing. In the name of pain in the name of confusion, of anger, pride, doubt, and so many other ideals that can stand in the way of every fragment we are meant to piece away from to know ourselves enough to love him. Especially for the home he created and intended for all of us to be united forever. That being said, sometimes I wonder about the angels that then in turn became demons, the ones that revel in it. In turning others away from God, in chaos, in anarchy, in death, and the impure of this world they breed. Do any of them feel remorse? Do any of them wish to go back to the home they left? Do any of them feel the way I had on my journey to losing myself in all the wrong? Do any of them regret what they did against him?

Is forgiveness possible to the ones who know they were dead wrong? Is there a hierarchy within even the angels who fell? Evil dwells among evil, but what of those that wish they had made the better choice? Could a demon pray? This is what we refer to all of them as, or are they truly all the same? Are they all a part of the dark that carried me away from God too? I wonder about them all. Maybe in a different way than most. I wouldn't dare play advocate to the devil, or ever choose the lesser of any evil, because that's still evil. Though I often think, can angels grieve the way we can? And of the angels that lost their graces; do their instruments inside of their chest sing out anything but demonic praises? Do any of them sing out regret like me? The saddest part about my pain was that it distorted my image. It pierced my heart from the inside out and I learned to walk behind my own shadow. I wonder if not just the angels in heaven for those they lost, but some on earth that lost themselves too, if they feel the same as I did.

    I keep mentioning time to all of you. But really what is time? It's not something I can touch. It's something we really can't see unless enough of it or not enough has passed. But what is it really? Why does time and the expectations of time become so unforgiving? Why are we only supposed to grieve for as long as the flowers last? Why did celebrating his life bask in the glory-lessness of his death? What I experienced with him felt like a portion of my own. Why wasn't I shielded from seeing it? Why did God want me to hold this affliction so gravely so that I carried it with me for the years to come. Is that God? Is this a part of his beautiful creation that became, no pun intended, but distorted over time as sin reared its ugliness to intertwine with good. Or is it the window peeking from the darkness that wingless angels stay, waiting through this ever hour in the corner with patience warped pride, for every illuminated soul's purity to fade like mine had. So the night of Papa's passing and how this leads to that boy in the royal blue sweatshirt collided.

Months passed after his death and for a time, I felt as if the human brain really had an auto-pilot button. I don't remember the days that followed weeks into months. Time just hurried and stopped all around me at the same moment. A breath of a season here and then it was gone. I barely remember sleeping. I don't think I did for a while. There were times I couldn't even feel sadness, I just felt gone like him. Sometimes my tears wouldn't fall. That felt like heartbreak all over again. Not even my tears could shed the pain away that clung to me with a passion. Maybe something was wrong with me. Even in school nothing really registered, and that boy turned into a blur of royal blue that I always felt a closeness to when I'd walk past. But this feeling bled into everything and nothingness at the same time. I never heard a word teachers or students would say. Despite the grief, and the sadness that would leave me empty or come back to leave me barely breathing, it was a break from the way teachers have always treated me. This I registered but mostly that no one said much and the silence that enveloped me felt like I was somehow cut off from the rest of the world. A touch away maybe from what death feels like. I hoped I would just fade away kind of like Papa had, and that somehow he was waiting for me to. It grieved me unconscionably that he went there alone. The darkest of thoughts swirled around in my mind, almost like when a tree branch bristles past your arm, or a leaf kisses your cheek in the wind. I felt the whispers festering as their volume got louder from something that resembled being behind me. It's a weird feeling to walk in black and white and feel nothing but gray. In my Lisa Frank childhood this was not something I had ever felt before, not even being sick or on death's door. This was deadly. That's how it felt to my heart. Then one day that gray turned into another color.

    I was sitting in class watching the clock and thinking about time, how much longer would I have of it without him. Something made me feel different in that moment. This dark rustling that always followed me, like my own personal storm cloud lifted a little. Not going too far away but not so close at the same time. I'm not sure how else to explain it. I felt a familiar feeling that I couldn't put a name to. I wondered, then I got up from my chair and walked to the door. Class was still active and kids were talking, the teacher may have been too. I didn't know why but something within me felt a magnified pull that needed to leave. I stared at the ground with confusion following my every step. I hesitated but walked away from the classroom, leaving some of the chatter behind. Following the distant whisper felt near but far away so I had to go after it. I looked up and I was met with another hug from the sun. Just like in the hospital with Papa. It brought me back to that memory, of me saying "hi stranger" and the look he gave me. I felt a pang in my chest but the sunlight wrapped around me tightly and the tears went away, not because they couldn't fall but because walking through that hallway something aside from the warmth caught my eye, and halted my grief to a dead stop. I saw the boy in the royal blue sweatshirt walking in the opposite direction, he looked at me but my tear forgiven eyes looked at him and then passed him. The pang in my chest ceased. It looked as if the sun was hugging him too. But my heart skipped when I saw them. The most beautiful sight I had ever seen. I saw angel wings behind him. I looked at them and then his face, he smiled at me and for the first time since before Papa's passing I smiled back.

It wasn't just at the time of grief and drowning in the unknown. It wasn't just confusion or deafening noise, it was my heart breaking. It just took the weeks and months that followed Papa's death for it to register that he was really gone and not coming back. Once after I then carried guilt. He always knew when I was sick or not feeling well, just by looking at me. The doctor that diagnosed him in the ER said that he must have had the cancer for at least four to five years because of how aggressive it was, and the size of the tumor when he found it. To know that he was suffering for so long and not understanding what it was. That made me feel so inadequate as his granddaughter. It made me feel so guilty, I could have helped him. I could have saved him, if I just knew somehow like he always knew with me. Then there was the only constant that I had before everything fell apart, a cute boy. Who would have known the angels saw this too. This beauty, that was a gift I hadn't realized then and I didn't know what to do with. Especially after seeing the most terrible sight, death in front of me. I saw something sent from heaven. The last take away, mind you I was just thirteen years old, I was convinced that the boy in the royal blue sweatshirt may have been an angel himself. You can laugh at me, I do when I think about it and every now and again. Then eventually over the next three years we would spend together passing each other in the hallways. I thought maybe it could have been Papa, or maybe it was his guardian angel. Maybe that boy lost someone close like I had, maybe both of our guardian angels shined that day. I wish I could have asked him. What happened made me remember how I felt before all the bad, it made me remember the girl I was before Papa died. Just from a smile, and of course those beautiful angel wings that looked like they were made from light. Some people are meant to come into our lives for a purpose. That boy became a symbol of hope that God knew I needed. Everything changed but that boy didn't. He stayed the same, and his smile did too. I never got to thank him for what he did for me that day. I never had the courage to tell him, to talk to him about it. What would I have said anyway, "hey I know you're an angel, thanks for showing me your wings". Maybe the way he helped me then when I needed it the most I can for him now. Maybe I can now show him mine, the ones that God gave me and marked onto my heart. Maybe he is reading this and if he is well,

To the boy in the royal blue sweatshirt,

Maybe we'll cross paths again, maybe in ten years or in the next lifetime and if and when we do I'll thank you. I hope until that time comes this book and the huge part you have within my journey to finding God is enough. I'll thank you for what you did to help that broken girl who couldn't feel anything but sadness could then feel your smile. I'll thank you for the emotions you exhumed out of me when I was at my lowest just by walking past me in that hallway. I'll thank you for the blessing it was to have known you the exact way I did and I'll tell you how I wouldn't have changed a single thing, not even one word. We'll reminisce about all the times I tried but failed to talk to you. We'll laugh about my silly imagination and the otherworldly war I thought would erupt because you may have been a nephilim and the secrets I would have kept for your protection. Maybe we won't say anything at all again, maybe we'll just walk past each other like we always have. Until the future I know God will reign true. I'll thank you then.

It's the little things in life that matter the most, when people go through grief they tend to attach themselves to what they are used to. For me I had nothing that was the same. The only comforts I ever knew were all gone. I was in a new house, a new town, a new school with a huge part of my heart missing. And then there was him. Who would have known the simplicity of my pain was what would have healed it in the end. All I was missing and had gained was the color blue.

Chapter Four
The Allure of Healing Painlessly

Prior to the ripping of my own heart out which will soon come in the next chapter. I was faced with this false security that the pain would cease, and that time was once again going to become my friend. How wrong I was. In this simulation of what a world would look like without Papa, that I'd somehow learn to be okay in. With the smile on my face that Papa loved so much and angel wings on my mind, what could have possibly hindered me from grieving Papa's death to the point that it wouldn't hurt me anymore? I know all too well how pain stays. Pain adheres to you and doesn't want to let you go. The hug you never asked for. I couldn't understand as young as I was how there was no ease with suffering. No way to breathe easier within or around it. Not with wounds so fresh and I learned even more so in the hardest ways as a little girl, not with scars either. Papa's death was nothing like I had ever experienced, I thought this pain would leave me. I couldn't have survived it if someone would have told me the torment I would still have yet to face. I didn't get the chance to settle in my hurt. The calm before the storm, there really wasn't one. Only the arms length distance of what it could have been. That darkness has a way of waging war, especially from the depths those that dwell in darkness will crawl away from in search of the soul they are after.

    The time that followed me after I saw those wings, I felt lighter, I didn't feel weighed down anymore by my grief, I felt like I could hold it and place it beside me when I wanted to let it go for a while. It was never long, that hurt would always beckon the warmth of my hands around it. But even then, I was just okay. Weeks passed, my sleeping wasn't getting any better. However the worlds of pain and time interlaced and my suffering was measured somehow. I'm not sure if it was by this world, the devil or by God himself. But it was determined within the suffering I had faced; until that point hadn't been enough. I didn't know what worse someone could feel, or what more someone could grieve and take. The human body can endure a lot. So can the human heart. But I would soon find out just how much. My Mom, as she was worried about me, talked about my grief from losing Papa to someone who he had called a friend. The doctor was a friend of the family and also a customer of Papa's too, he had cut his hair for years. It was then he turned to look at me and his secretary who I had also known since I was just a baby. The look on his face he had at that moment I attributed to hope. I thought that's what his eyes reflected back to me. The one thing I was craving but didn't know how else to see unless it was the boy in the royal blue sweatshirt's eyes looking back into mine. How wrong I was. I learned early on patience can be warped into pride. Well I would then soon find out that hope can be distorted into depravity. When these things occur hope and patience are snuffed out in place of their evil counterparts. It's a sadness that washes over the parts of you that may never be clean again. I wonder if that's how angels feel about the souls they lose. The one who doesn't find their way back to God because of what the demons carve out to sin with the mangle and broken parts of those that used to be good. Maybe some of us still are, but yet this can happen. My tears turned into the rainsong that the demons danced to and that is when heaven mourns what can happen with freewill. When the darkness surrounds you extinguishing the light and you don't know any better. What I had made in the face of sin. A creation of more pain and wounds to my soul. If only I saw the face that I needed to; God's. If only I had known him then. Thus, the consequences trailed because I lacked the knowledge of who he was. The world took hold of me and I looked into the face of sin until I saw it looking back at me in the mirror. Balance is needed in everything. I saw sickness, and pain my whole childhood only to watch death's cry. Then I saw those beautiful wings, of course it was evil's turn again to steal more than just my health or sight this time.

So in the lull that followed such beauty. In the delicateness of being able to remove my hurt and place it in a box beside me. Time rained on and I started to try. I put the little things in a place where I could reach for when I wanted to feel that way again. The joy he would always bring me, but now it wasn't alone, sorrow was joined at the hip. I put the pictures and lotto tickets, Papa's sunglasses and more things that reminded me of him in an old cologne box of his. I even saved his favorite gum wrapper. The little parts of him that I got to hold onto. It was almost unfathomable the man he was, with such heart and such character; I could dare to fit my memoires in such a place that seemed to make me feel small too. It made me feel so displaced in my role of being his princess. Of being the one grandchild he raised. It made me feel inconsequential, it made me feel like that box wasn't there for me to use to remember him, but for me to use to take the weight of my hurt and dump it onto him. That just made my hurt grow even more. So on the shelf of my closet it would go, or underneath by bed. Places that were near but far enough away from me where I wouldn't have to carry it. That made me internalize this notion as no longer wanting to carry him. No longer wanting to love him. It made me think he thought I hated him. He left me, and I didn't know what to do with all that he had left behind. My memories became this hall of paintings and pictures of splendor that were sharp to the touch and even serrated to the sight. My memories began to weigh on me, so one by one and picture by picture I used that box not for the stuff, but for my own heart when I didn't want it to beat to the rhythm of his endless stall which meant for it not to beat at all. Then the cascade of dark thoughts erupted in and around my mind. Almost like someone else had put them there. I thought maybe he wasn't meant to go alone. I certainly wasn't meant to be forsaken and on my own. Not in this world. This little bubble of heaven Papa bear had made just for me. That home. It was all gone. Time changes all things, but at the same time the constant stays the same. It was a hardship to endure, Nonna, Mom and I all had to face it in our own ways, on our own. Slowly things started to shift. Things I wasn't used to. Like going to the shop, that was gone long before his passing, but it was another addition of home, and that was gone too. There was no other safe ground to stand on. We were in this new place, a supposed home but not at all. Even going outside the air seemed different. Maybe it just seemed that way, but I remember how sad it made me. The wind seemed to blow less at this new place. I was expected to consider something that didn't resemble home and even more so call it that. I've never known any home without stucco in the front, or arches on the porch. This new house didn't have either, I also never knew a home without the dreamland the backyard could become if the sun was just right, with Papa cooking on the grill, and the flowers climbing around the spotlights in a race to try and kiss the sky. I never knew a home that didn't have a secret passageway from the woods leading to the magical lands, though I was always too scared to venture that far. But I just knew what fairytales lay past those fallen branches and old pool cover. It's the saddest thing; losing time. You lose so much even when you gain things to replace what's gone. It's not the same. God really does prune away at what we need to lose. It can be messy, painful and even the sky can feel like it's falling too. But he does this to teach us, to form us, to bend us not to just his will but our own. This freewill he gave to us, it's free but it's costly. God gave us his will, little portions of it that we then can use to hurt or heal. To maim or to nurture. We choose in the end. For me, the end always seemed not far, but I've been proven wrong countless times. I sometimes would fear when Papa would tell me I would get better. Some small doubt inside of me would taunt my riddled little body with the idea that maybe one day I wouldn't. I was wrong thankfully, I did get better. Every time. I was wrong again when I thought that box would solve all my problems. I thought wrong when the pain of losing Papa and the dust that felt like it wouldn't settle, did. It just settled around me, it was my hurt that painted this target on my heart. It was as if I had been marked by the devil himself. It's this one, this one girl who needs to suffer more. How interesting, being that I really never knew my creator and through all the pain and all the trials, it wasn't until after I defeated them all that I got to meet him at the finish line. I was cured and preserved by my pain, if not for the pain and suffering in this world how could we really know and behold what God went through? How could we measure our own suffering if we don't learn to measure his? Sometimes the end isn't so. Sometimes time doesn't heal any wounds, sometimes time creates them and in doing so creates us to the fullest potential of the person and the will we are meant to reflect.

So as time went on, I would go through the day trying to leave that pain behind me. It followed me nonetheless but I pretended like I couldn't hear it, couldn't feel it. I went from class to class, holding my breath through the pain of it all. I would dread the time where nothing would happen. Even though I couldn't hear the teachers, it was the noise that I could drown my hurt into, even through the stifled sounds. Always reliving those last moments with him. My mind always brought me back to that one moment, not his last breath; that would come later. It was a blur to me at this point. But the warmth that flooded around us, seeing him in that wheelchair, the look he had and then the memory of him coming home sitting in the car. How happy I had been to see him, and the hurt that was on both our faces when I did. I just went in whatever direction time wanted me to go in. Even walking passed the boy in the royal blue sweatshirt couldn't keep the nightmares my waking eyes would drudge from my subconscious away. Though those were the highlights of my grief. The points where the warmth would hug me all around even my pain lessening the intensity of it completely. That one blur of blue made my heart smile, especially when closing my eyes all I'd see was a blur of red. I thought this meant I was healing nonetheless. That summer of not seeing him everyday was the hardest.

That friend of the family Mom talked to about my grief, he had an idea about me working for him. I'd start in the summer and then work the weekends during the school year. It was going to be good for me. This was what had been foretold. My Mom believed it. Believed him. And so did I. So when the school year ended and I no longer had that boy to catch the pieces falling from my heart, I thought that being around more constant and what was familiar would help. The people I knew, someone Papa trusted, would push the grief away, maybe even more than an angel could have because Papa would have been proud of me like Mom and Nonna were. I wish they had been right. I wish I had been right too. But more than that, I wish Papa hadn't died. I wished he could have saved us both from the deaths we succumbed to in our end.

Chapter Five
Death of Me

I thought something might have been wrong with me, another sort of sickness. I had such sadness, but my tears wouldn't fall. Very sparingly did they ever after Papa's passing. So when this new way of coping came into the picture, I thought better of my tearless sorrow. I thought maybe I didn't need them after all. More noise to drown away the hurt, I welcomed the idea. Once after the arrow aimed for my soul was punctured by this insidiousness, not even the crying of my heart was loud enough to ring out sound for him to hear. Not because he couldn't, but because he didn't care to acknowledge it's mourning. Not just for my agony, or my breaking apart. My very being felt like it was fading away. I was being crumpled up and eroded by the will of a sinful man. I felt as if Papa's soul was being desecrated with mine. This sting of the wicked, especially when you don't know any better echos. I was always kept safe in my bubble, then one day I was brought to a place where the word safe itself hung in the balance. It didn't seem necessary for that word to be questioned as to the validity of what variation safe meant. To the baseness of one individual. One person's weaknesses. One man's inability to not harm, or keep his hands to himself. That's what it took for the detriment of a girl like me. The girl I used to be anyway. The girl I was before more darkness bled into the tragedy already surrounding me, now becoming me. The girl that cried out of fear for the shadows that peaked through the moonless skyless void and now wondered if she should welcome it instead. I was torn in two after losing Papa. But after the world chipped away at me through the guise of time, I began to lose parts of myself. The parts that I clung to. The parts of me that still knew how to hope. Until he took them away and shattered them before me. My mind let him become a scarier monster then the ones I let hold my hand where my hurt used to stay. Numbness enveloped me whole and I didn't fight it. I raised my own hand in the destruction of her too. I didn't realize until after all those years of being ostracized and ridiculed, it taught me how to do the same but to the girl I'd turn away from in the mirror. I never weeped for more or less beauty, I never wished on stars for a smaller or skinnier waist. Yet mirrors started to cry for me the tears I couldn't and then only after my tears learned to fall like the angels did. I followed not long after this time had passed through me. After that man foamed at the mouth at the cirrus of my innocence. That truly became the start of the death of me.

Chapter Six
Consequence of Pain

What is left after the start of every fairytale? The slow burn of evil's upper hand. The one evil that inevitably takes hold of those that haven't been taught that word yet. Maybe some have heard it or read about it. Up until that point I had experienced sickness, fear, trauma, and even witnessed death. But evil wasn't something that I understood. I experienced hurt, pain, and affliction from others. But I never knew evil unless it was a dark figure holding an apple in a book somewhere. I never knew evil until the fear and anxiety I learned to keep over time surrounding doctors, then took a turn and reflected the same doom I had always feared lay in wait underneath my bed at night. The monsters that stay in the dark corners of the kitchen or in my closet. I couldn't comprehend the idea that the monsters that were never really there, and this I knew; but the questionability of what if always dancing around my mind. I was not ready for those fears to become my reality and have what became the scariest of monsters that ever pulled fear out of me materialize.

There stood eyes locked on the ill immaculate inception of the girl I would no longer be because of him. I couldn't comprehend how evil could look so human. I didn't know evil could even be human. I had known people to be cruel, even those who weren't supposed to be. That I couldn't understand alone, but this I just couldn't see. Even with what stood before me. I didn't know a man with a beating heart like mine could warrant such evil. Someone who could feel pain like I could, like everyone else, could then turn around to inflict it onto others. I never had a shred of an idea that people you trust could turn around and break it. I wasn't well versed on what evil really was at all. This world has so much of it, by the choices people make. This man made many choices of evil descent. The little morsels of what the apple symbolized was nothing to the veracity of what evil can actually measure. Evil isn't alone, it's wrapped in different packaging. What is evil? I found out. It's the freewill to choose, but to choose wrong. It's to choose sin.

My butterfly wings that were mangled was the worst part of the insidiousness that surrounded my vulnerability. It wasn't just from the grief I inherited bearing witness to a death. This bared parts of my soul and the spotlessness of my butterfly wings to the devil. Those wings that Papa gave me, not in his death but in his life. I was many things to him but farfallina was one that rang the softest to my ears. So when that doctor started to cut holes in them, it was as if Papa was being cut right alongside me.

Trust is like a rose. Beautiful to look at, to be near, to embrace as its scent wraps around you delicately. You have to know how to behold something that divine. Especially with its thorns climbing the incandescence of the same question I posed many times, what if? To have embedded in its glory, a natural defense mechanism. It's a wonder why we aren't all more careful. Hasn't nature's story been foretold for thousands of years? Not just the beauty of it but the brutality of it too. Let's all be brutally honest not for the sake of being brutal, but of just being honest. Defense in nature is a constant, always, not just for the adverse consequences of being prey vs being predator. But what happens when we take nature's ever battlefield and apply it to everyday human life. We get a sad lost little butterfly whose wings lose flight from the terror of being prey but entrusting her mend with someone who became predator, monster, but more than anything else just another human who sinned gravely. When is it measured, those that sin, and those that sin against someone else? Does some echo of the grief sound somewhere? Can God hear it the way the devil did? Yes.

    The little butterfly with tattered wings began to shed the hurt parts of herself, the loss and confusion, but then she began to shred and prune away at the good parts too. Innocent turned meek. She cocooned in her hurt, what had been given to her and what she then inflicted onto herself and she became the little lamb who stifled her cries and wiped her tears on the barbed wire of her fear. She welcomed it and mourned it at the same time without realizing the skull of the dead isn't something to belove. It's not something to dread either. It's something to stomp on. So this little lamb suffered, graveled and bled. She whimpered and cried for mercy all the while the choices and decisions she made were godless to cope with the trauma. Naive in the measurements of them, yes. But still where there is no light there is no hope.

Eventually it became apparent to the pain, not to me that I could no longer place it beside me any more. I had to hold it's hand while the darkness called out to me sickly-sweet and autopilot no longer was in the driver's seat. Sin wrapped around the gift box of Pandora was. How dazzling sin can look for some when you first meet. It's a bitterness you get used to and eventually learn to crave.

Chapter Seven
The Undoing That Was Choosing Good or Evil

A choice is what led to my annihilation that spread to the iris of the sparks that used to shine within and around my heart to burn out. It was also a hindrance that led to my own destruction. The bits and pieces he had missed or forgot to hurt, it was left for me to smother out. To extinguish the flickers of light that I hadn't lost when Papa died. The tiny fragments that floated around, that I then held or placed in that box haunted me. Until the darkness conveyed ideas of turning them into weapons to hurt my pain instead. That only hurt me more. Of course this notion of an idea was sold to me as healing. I had fallen sick many times before, too many to count. I had felt the cast of death when its shadow walked past mine to reach out for Papa's and take him away. I felt the sting and burn of my wounds being excised by demons under the guise of angel energy.

A granule of hope, a sliver of whatever was opposite of how I was feeling I had been chasing endlessly. And so through the broken glass I crawled not knowing it was more than just the broken pieces of myself I was trampling over thinking those were what was going to save me. I had the right idea, but the worst application. The brokenness I held closer than the whole parts I was searching for and losing more of at the same time. I didn't know it was God I had been searching for all along, I didn't know him then, only barely of him. But in my haste and impatience of wanting the key to the end of this suffering, not realizing my suffering was the key. I turned away from the broken glass, embers and ash of the flame that used to burn bright inside my chest; towards the fire from the dark that hissed my name. In my inexperience, towards the devil. The ideal of who he "is", it didn't register to me. Only what he "was", until it was too late. Not comprehending the dark wraps around the devil's fingers much like playing the harps strings but inside his own chest cascading a deadly hymn. It's a notion that can sting not only the air around you, but who you are when you no longer reflect the person you once were. When you become your own worst enemy and the parts of yourself that were once good becomes a distant memory. In the arms of, not God's, but instead I was enveloped around the wingless angel in the blur of looking for my own variation out of harm's way. All the while I placed myself right in the middle of it. The imprint and burn that scrawled deep toward my soul was the consequence of my mourning grievously. I mourned Papa. I was now mourning myself.

Not understanding what evil was before, I now knew, so I had thought. I thought evil only lay within death. I had the weight to carry with me now. The chains around my arms and legs invisibly pulling my inhibitions down with the reality of what was really happening. What I was really losing. So I learned and bent to the beckoning call of a flower that could somehow hold the answers no one else could foretell. I convinced myself the deeper the lengths I'd go to grasp a hold of some faith, the better I'd be. The less I'd suffer. I didn't realize then what I had invoked, and who I had shunned. Through the thick of this agony things started happening and not all were dark. Most were, but those fleeting gleams of who had been walking beside me all along sounded too. I just couldn't hear it yet. The devil may have instruments inside his chest, and those were the notes I followed blindly. But every now and then I'd turn my head back to hear the percussion something deep inside me would foresee before my eyes could, of the lion roaring from inside God's.

Light peeking through the clouds of my pain was God. If only I would have recognized it. That's how I became a writer. Through the midst of me being lost not just to God, and to myself. I even started to become lost to the devil. God called out to me many times when I couldn't hear or see. I started writing when I first lost Papa. Two words, a name on a crumpled piece of paper was what started it all. The year that followed was now that of my death. This became the height of all the pain that wouldn't let me go. Amazingly enough certain parts of it not even the demons could touch. I started writing, it helped me, maybe even started to heal me. But I had already welcomed the darkness prior, so once the raised parts of my wounds started to become clean. The darkness roamed and I with it. The writing turned dark too. My talent was being tainted without my understanding. The gift God gave me, being used to mock him and I both.

Prior to the start of my writing however, this was another gift God had given me in the very beginning of what would be my own crucifying. I wasn't just rifling through the broken parts of myself. I was looking through the parts that used to hope. I thought maybe I could hang onto them. Since it was Papa's hand I could no longer hold. I drifted with the idea of faith, but it was more searching ruthlessly and endlessly for what could fill the hole that was left in my heart. The first time I fell away, I was looking for something I could connect with through the pain of Papa no longer being here. So buddha statues seemed to be what garnered my attention, the lotus flower first and the "spirituality" of buddhism quickly followed suit. This being said, a book about meditations in regards to flowers and statues of buddha heads from marshalls seemed to be the slightest approach of blasphemous naiveness that didn't turn or harm me in the tenfold manner the other things I found did. I had felt like God, though I never knew him failed me, left me behind, and took Papa away. Then shortly after the span of months with buddha statues adorning my bedroom another tragedy struck. My own. So when this "faith" too had "failed me", I then looked elsewhere. Quickly changing my faith and interchanging the ground I'd stand on when my pain would come back harsher than when it would leave me. So through the book store I wandered searching for someone, something to take my pain away. To stop it. Because pain, being painful; I didn't want to feel it anymore. I didn't want it to know me so intrinsically like it did. I wanted to be free, but bound was how I'd end up by the free choices I made to be exonerated from the sentence suffering can issue. I didn't want to lose anymore of myself, but I would.

Even the word faith had become more decoration than something for me to hold onto. The further we go away from God as a society, this is what can happen. Ornaments of the words and gifts from the bible and God himself become empty, not because they are. But because we no longer hold them with the weight, or teach about the true measure they give. What is faith if not a sign from a decor store or a cute word on a bracelet? What is it truly? God would show me but only after stepping into the fire like I had that the devil bore to me through witchcraft and alienating what was missing within myself towards anarchy. If the question would have been presented to me even through pain, naiveness and confusion, I'd like to think I would have chosen wisely. But what is even wisdom without knowing Christ?

Chapter Eight
Rendition of Responsibility

What is the responsibility of pain? What is the responsibility of grief? What is one supposed to do with wounds they cannot heal on their own, and time itself becomes an adversary? What is the direction to take to not hemorrhage from suffering? When does the rendition of responsibility to agony bleed into the choices and vices those fall to thinking would heal? What is the emergence of heeding the warning that being in pain and loss can echo? Why aren't we taught about death but more so how it can cut those around it? Who is in control when sorrow blinds every sense someone can have to push towards the danger vulnerability and hurt can resound? Who can be faulted by not understanding and distinguishing between good and evil? What is the rubric for those who weren't introduced to God in the way that could have saved them from all the confusion? What about the choices some will be led to inevitably without him? What are the side effects from being educated about God in minute doses and never being introduced to the devil in necessary spouts of wariness? The devil's biggest ploy is to convince people that he doesn't exist. I never knew of him either. I only knew of people being mean, or eventually I would see evil not knowing of the word itself. I never knew God the way I would personally be known by the devil. I was known by God too. It just took me walking through the fractured smoke and mirrors that lay to waste before me, for all of it to clear so I could. Or maybe it was my eyes that needed to drudge through the wreckage, not my soul even though that's what felt like had. In what ways can we be prepared to lose ourselves? It's not a matter of if, it's a matter of when. There were many things I've learned through my vocation of suffering and one of the biggest secrets most don't realize; suffering is a part of this world no matter who you are. It's almost a right of passage toward holiness. Not everyone who is holy has to suffer. Not everyone has to suffer for the sake of being holy. But God suffered. We have the gift of freewill. We ultimately decide. When it came to our salvation God sent us his son. So it makes sense to me years later, the woman I am now writing this compared to the lost girl I had been without Christ and only had pain. Eventually it was more pain I would hold onto and seek without knowing that's what I was doing. I fear for those that have yet to go through the cycle of grief but for themselves, and their own personal losses and mourning of that word. Will. To understand in the truest of ways we have to understand his suffering. Not just read about it and study it. We have to mourn it also and precisely understand the suffering he endured. For some suffering is a necessity for this notion alone. Not to mention the vices, evils, and false deities within these cosmos. It is and through suffering people will find God. I did. For others it can be sickness, ailments, and agony that pushes one to pray. This isn't the greater argument for the sake of suffering and how it's necessary. It's a rendition of the responsibility within and around the way our world is. There is balance, there is good and evil. There is freewill to freely choose. Whatsmore, there is redemption, and beauty in pain. Not for the sake of being beautiful but of being refined within God's sacred heart so we can amass the tools to curate our own through the broken pieces that will make us whole. This then leads to the idea of fault. Was it my fault, the darkness that I seeked out and followed without properly understanding the totality of it? Was it my fault the evils that not only I sought, but those that were done against me? In what echo chamber does sin gravitate? Is it through the neglect of who we are and what we are capable of surviving? When suffering ferments it leads ultimately to more, until you realize the power within using your pain for good. This would take me many years after my grief to believe this as truth. Prior to my testimonial of endurance, I also have a testimonial of devilry. The rendition of my torment that became the symphony the demons would make with parts of me that would die away through the idea that died within me first. Into the abyss of dark I went, tottering away from the only thing I wanted most, the iridescence of light. Instead the breaking that happened to my mind was what it was like for me to bear the wound of sin.

Chapter Nine
Breaking to Heal

I had to break to heal. But it was through that breaking that I felt the good vilified through my own eyes but distorted through the shadow of lies. It's harsh when things like the odious take root. It becomes a part of your new world view of everything that is wrong somehow beckons the idea that it's right. The entirety of your morality shifts. For some, like myself this shift wasn't felt immensely. I didn't have the foundation to glorify God the way I started to with the devil. I didn't know how to glorify the good enough. Instead I could only see what was homage to the bad. I wish I would have been able to shake that young girl into discernment before the torment really began. Before the pour of scorn turned inward as the balm to my wounds that demons cut to ribbons and I not only let, but helped them to my own decay.

It wasn't the beauty of my pain I started to recognize and use, that came with God. It was the illusion of beauty to the chaos of my pain I learned to hunger for from the devil. I want to share with you all, a small excerpt from my diary when this took place:

> "I am continuously forming thunder clouds and lightning from the thoughts I can not get shelter from, it's a storm that never subsides and yet a beautiful one at that."

This was written when I was nineteen years old. It felt like the anxiety being the constant that it became, would never go away. There were piercing moments where it's almost as if I didn't want it too. This of course wasn't that of my own accord. No, this was the decry from the demons plaguing around me that I had the silliest of notions weren't anything but fallen angels. But of a different kind. This on some level I knew. It wasn't what I felt from the "hi stranger" memory with Papa. And it most certainly wasn't the feeling that came with the boy in the royal blue sweatshirt either. This was different. A variation of angels. A variation to healing. A darkness enveloped until it was no longer around me, but within me.

This is when it became clear which "side" I was on. It wasn't God's. I would even have said as much. With words that felt like a hot iron, unnatural and ill to say. Yet the emotions and feelings behind them confused me even more than these alluded thoughts. It was as if this angst I was feeling was from someone else. These words that I didn't understand and these sentiments that seemed to be placed on me. They didn't come from my broken heart. I'm not even sure if they came from my broken mind. I think they came from the brokenness of the demons; I think that's why they attack in a certain rhythm and pattern toward the meek and tender. I think it was because even though it pains me to say. We had something in common. It's a heavy shame that I carry. The load loses its weight everytime I pray, or spread God's light to someone in passing. It helps to go to confession and receive the eucharist. But more so than all of that glory; it's when I sit in a local church right next to the sacred heart of Jesus sacramental. There's something about Jesus' hand to his bleeding heart wrapped with the barbed wire of pain and yet light exudes from him. That I can recognize all these years later, that I had something in common with my creator too. Though my heart no longer bleeds like it used to. Time is a funny thing. It comes and goes from friendship, enemy and something in between all too quickly. It became apparent that time itself isn't evil, or good. It's utterly benevolent but within being okay and perpetual torment it can aid within pulling you to pieces. It's a sadness that should be stigmatized but isn't, that's why not a lot of people know about it until it's too late. I myself became my own worst enemy. Nothing or no one could have prepared me for the exalted way in which I went about the detriment to my soul. This heartache and guilt I still stifle.

So it wasn't just for the rabbit holes that existed all around calling my name. They did but it was elsewhere that the demons beckoned for a more appropriate way for me to hinder. The zeal of creativity called. So the rabbit holes were not for me. That would have been too simple. Not enough responsibility on my shoulders that the devil wanted me to convey and carry. So under construction I went to the floor plans of my own martyrdom. I think it was in this very way of being the mastermind behind my own suffering, it's within this that the devil was at play. I really needed to understand how and why I had to face the persecution of my own silly judgment. To play judge, jury, and executioner to my pain when it wasn't my pain I was trying to blot out. It was me. All of me. The devil despises the purity of the lamb, the same way the demons shudder at the roar of the lion. I had once been a butterfly and shed and morphed into a little lamb. It was at this measure where I would stay. It wasn't until after God I would become something completely different in its entirety.

"Mary lost a little lamb"

It grieves me till this day. When I look back and see behind those moon painted eyes the little lamb I had become. Prey for predators. I wasn't just the girl with stiff joints and agony that had such depths that seas of the world couldn't go deep enough to resemble. Little lamb I had become wasn't just the picked out parts of her innocence, whether it had been by other kids, teachers, doctors, and people far and yet near so that's how they hurt her. How people can be physically here but mentally gone, I never understood until it was me at the other end of this certain kind of pain. The kind inflicted by others. When it was me at the end of a sharp remark, the other end of a disparaging lecture or at the other end of profanity spewed to inflict its curse within my heart. The other end of sickness too, or even at the other end of death. The other end of sin. It wasn't until that little lamb became lost within her being lost that the arrows she pulled out from her sides and chest she then used to turn around and condemn the healed parts so they would open and bleed once again so they could feel like she did. I wasn't just the girl with a heavy heart, and a tenderness to those who always caused me more pain. The little lamb who held forgiveness within her swollen hands and broken hurt. She was the little lamb Mother Mary lost before she knew who she was. The little lamb that would leave this world everynight in her mind and pull those dreams that cured into prayers closest to her redemption so she could visit the clouds and sleep with the angels; so the grief of her still being gone to herself wouldn't seem like the open wound it still was." So the little lamb was lost until she found him. Until really God found her.

But prior to God finding her, and the little gifts of breath he would send without me realizing; this is where I departed from the flock. This is when I openly choose to follow the devil and play advocate to the pain he inflicted that I then used to inflict onto myself seven times over.

So down the forbidden path of welcoming tarot cards, and asking for answers to those who are all too aperitive to give. This should have been the biggest warning I could have received. But nope, not even predicting death on three different occasions could have thwarted the ideal that I started to sustain within my misguided "I knew best" perception. No matter how it would shred away within my mind. No matter that it would keep me up at night. No matter the crippling anxiety or panic attacks. No matter the absolute terrier that became just another thing for me to carry. I was used to carrying suffering. I have since I was a baby. This took root around my cleanness and drenched me in the grime of my own choices. It was similar to after Papa died, I felt like my brain had pushed the auto-pilot button but different. Yet it was also similar to the desecration of my butterfly wings, the painstaking reality as to why I didn't have them anymore. I wish I would have at least learned to fly while I did. But that couldn't be helped when a man that could hold not only my own, but my family's trust right inside his back pocket. Similar, yet different also. Any and every time I had been tarnished by another person, it left its mark. It left a stain that just eventually became a part of my image. The scars from doctors and hospitals added to this image. The emotional scourging since a little girl added to this as well. It felt like it was a divine interception of my pain.

My suffering was creating something that I couldn't see or feel but laminate in. This is when the clock struck midnight to the path I jaggedly walked. Always zig zagging away but near Christ. Even without knowing him. He knew me. Those little detours took a harsh corner and the light within my very being burned out. That's when the dark flame of ache grew. Almost as if the colorlessness around me became brighter than even the only one I clung to.

This was something else that took part, another something beautifully tragic to add within and around this smoldering. When Papa passed away the color within the fairytales I could muster died. Then slowly that notion began to proliferate around me and color started to bleed out of my world like Papa had. I think this is why one color stayed behind. It wasn't just the boy who wore it. It became a blur for time within my teary eyes. I think this was God too. It's hard to sift through the broken from the unbroken. Especially when you can't see the whole picture. When you can't see yourself in it. I think it's an interesting mustard seed of an alms that the demons didn't seem to notice walking with me just like they did. These new feelings and pangs of loss that I felt during this time of calamity, I was using my outstretched arms like wings the angels had; just to lose them in the same way I started to piece them together. Broken shards of my mind and soul couldn't sustain my creation. Building a foundation on anything but God and this is what happens. It felt like a death of a death. I slowly started to hear the chorus and orchestra of the demonic victory. It became too obvious to an extent and eventually they didn't even try to hide it. I started to peek behind the curtain and when I could help it, when I could separate the paranoia, the fear, the drowning sadness from the truth. That's when I started to really pick out the gravel and dirt in my wounds. The nightmares from hell didn't like that very much. The devil even more so hated it. There was this fleeting moment that lasted a time, where I don't think it was the devil pressing his trace on me. I think within the tide turning, and this bridge that the dark clouds covered I eventually started to see through. But I would have to cross that bridge. I think it was God, pricking my conscious in the end. I think it was the new overwhelming terror that was a gift. He gave me doubt and I began to see good or evil. That's when I decided in that one moment where both 'freedoms' lay before me. It took minutes or seconds, but time began to circle around me and I didn't meet it with haste. I didn't meet time with anger or hurt either. I met it with conviction. This feeling I hadn't felt before. Mixed with untainted fear. Fear from the devil is bitter, addicting and razor edged. Fear from God is not to maim, but to incorrupt. Fear of the Lord is a gift. At this very moment I think I shuttered not just from the realization that was being openly conveyed before me. I trembled recognizing this fear, a memory pierced my mind to an open door, I stared at the door in my bedroom as the next impact formed. I think I shook next because I heard the battle end. It was almost an immediate departure of "noise" then all that was left was a different kind of fear. Discernment. Not one that would fester to hurt me I somehow knew. But it would stay to help me until it didn't need to anymore. I again knew this somehow. I immediately ran to Nonna and asked her for a bible.

It was a grueling battle that took so many pieces of me, but this would only prepare me for the warfare ahead. A beautiful one. Shedding the decay I thought had now become a part of me. It really became like a war, to rip away at the darkness that wanted to adhere to my wounds and not depart from me. It was amazing how easy it had been to fall down the hill of morality, but it was near impossible to climb back up it to find my graces again I felt undeserving of when I left them behind. I could not have done it without God being with me every step of the way.

The mockery that had been made of my talents, it was a constant flight of energy to get back to the heart of what God had given me. I created many things and ultimately like the devil, chaos was what had been inbred. Yet I held great renounce to wanting to put my name on things that the world just didn't need more of. So I pushed all those characters and stories in the recess of my mind that sin would soon stay.

There was one character that I had such a connection to. She was the first character I had ever created. It was almost as if pushing Silver Moon into the world was not my own dream but my agony's. It took many points and time to grief her, but I ultimately let her go. I almost wonder if this is what the devil felt when I finally saw these evils I was surrounded by for what they really were. I can only say that I hope it broke his wretched heart worse than how my choices by his yearning broke mine. "The enemy thought he had me, but Jesus said you are mine." In my brokenness I created more brokenness. Yet, I just didn't want to give the world more darkness when that was how I felt what writing was like since the age of fifteen. From that point until the age of twenty. I hadn't just pressed the reset button on this life in how I would live it. I freely and openly choose the good. I chose God. So I departed from evil, and that is the biggest testament to how the little faith I had started with was restored in the same instance I felt like it was being given to me for the first time. I worked tirelessly and I think God did too to heal me. He healed me so much that he even healed my writing.

Chapter Ten
The Releasing of a Dove

Through the kaleidoscope of her hurt she began to learn how to refract light towards the wounds within; not to restore but to illuminate for others to heal by them. Thus began my next vocation of spreading God's light. The one that she became.

Through the haze of letting go of all that I had clung to for years, it wasn't a simple task. It wasn't easy. Far from it. It was an ease to be able to finally see straight. But it almost felt like despair I was losing to not be afraid anymore. To not have panic attacks or anxiety surround me like they had for so many years. To not worry myself sick. It was a reprieve and the gift it was, made my heart swell with relief yet parts of my mind were mournful of this gift too. This gift I knew was from God. This I did not understand though. I had been so accustomed to the pain it became the only constant I could rely on. Almost as if I mourned the sadness. I almost felt the heartbreak of wanting it to stay. I think the unknown was something I was used to within the bad. But the unknown of what is within the good I had never been able to hold onto for long. Once in a blue moon would the tips of my fingers be able to caress the trace of better health, or the aid to necessitate hurt thrown at me. It was daunting to remove the sin colored glass from my eyes and learn not to bleed anymore. "Diamonds are formed under pressure, and bread dough rises when you let it rest." God helped me through this new found level of torment. It was a pain but a good pain. It didn't bear its same sting, from what all the different versions I had mastered through felt like.

 I started to heal. It's amazing to say, and it wasn't something even within the unknown I had expected. My mind didn't look like the mangled trauma of dejection it had for so long anymore. I started to purge away at all the vices, the worldly lies, and falsehoods I had promised myself would save me in the end. Disillusion is a different kind of beast to fight through. Thanks be to God I could. So through the ways my pain echoed and light refracted back to the demons, I beat it all. I beat anxiety. I beat fear. I beat Ptsd. I beat the paranoia. I beat insomnia. I beat the terror. I beat the loneliness. I beat the devil. I found my way back; light peeked through the sky and iridescent clouds of my pain lessening towards hope, towards strength restored, towards healing, towards God and an open door. I started to sustain the life I thought I didn't want anymore.

Chapter Eleven
Falling to Grace

Through the door; bruises wrapped in light peaked behind my mind and I started to write about fairy tales again. Just like the ones I would always create in the one place I had loved so much. Home. It's amazing the cascading of God himself that can bore into one piece of paper and one pen, let alone through and around the person writing and the place where the magic of heaven descends. It was this fairytale that kissed those bruises away. Brushing away the tears of a little girl who clung to her Lisa Frank stationary like it would save her. My soul began to learn how to smile again. And so the death of Silver Moon was grieved tearless and with a peaceful disposition. So the timing was essential and Sweetpea was born.

Silver Moon was a character I created to help escape and also revel in the pain. Sweetpea is a character I created to soften the marks of pieces being put back together of my entire being. Silver Moon was a witch. Sweetpea is a light fairy. Still basking in the glories of other worldly things but it's a testament to both girls I became through suffering, one with displacing it and the other with saving it. My grace. I fell back toward the face of God, for the first time. Light shined through my creations, and I let Sweetpea take the place in my heart that Silver Moon wasn't ever supposed to. I choose to not just as a writer but as the girl herself not revel in the pain but use it like God did. I choose to not just yearn and behold the good, I learned to reflect it, to inspire it. And now I learned to spread it like any other disciple would.

Chapter Twelve
The Resurrection of Me

So everyone, it's been a whirlwind writing this book. I still have much more beauty to share with you all. But I want to highlight the most enamoring gift God has ever given me to date. This book isn't just a testimonial to all the bad that I've struggled with and faced throughout my life. The biggest, most important points are of the miracles God has shown and given me.

I not only turned my face toward my creator. I not only learned to shine light in the dark. I learned to fight, to forgive. I learned to endure and to suffer. I learned to measure my pain and my heart with it. I also learned to measure my healing. God gave me many things in this life. Until the three years that followed my pursuit of him. I leaned heavily into my experience, talents and created many things, stories, and characters. But more so I learned to be faithful. I learned to pray. I learned to study and read scripture, I started to heed not the warnings but the gifts that come with Christ. The love that he truly is and reflects to those who love him and obey him. I learned to become disciplined. I learned to not mourn my hurt and be thankful for it. I learned what it was to be whole again. I learned what it felt like to not fear anymore. I learned what it was for the first time in my entire life to be a girl without Juvenile Rheumatoid Arthritis.

God healed me of many things. He came for my soul to be renewed. He came back for me. After all the terrible I had naively clung to. He healed me of all my pain. This is where my fermenting ended. I began a new vocation; spreading God's light through the reflection of my heart just like his. This is what led to me creating a space online to teach bible study. (Sunday Brunch) This is what led me to finally being done with all the battles and wars. None lay before me now, and even if some did they aren't any I can't conquer. Praise to you Lord Jesus Christ.

Many thanks and apologies come to mind;

I'm sorry to my guardian angel, I'm sorry for almost never acknowledging your presence. I'm sorry for losing the many battles we both faced that I didn't know were together. I'm sorry if your light dimmed as the demons and sin alighted my eyes through nothing but the dark. I'm sorry for the grief you faced, the hurt or pain of me walking away. I'm sorry for the tears and songs you shed for my innocence departing. I'm sorry for the death of me. I'm sorry I didn't know how to breathe back into my wounds anything but more pain. I'm sorry it took me so long to know about you. I'm sorry the devil had me in his grasp. I'm sorry for turning my cheek away from our creator. I'm sorry for your loneliness. I'm sorry for the moments you thought you might never get me back. I'm sorry for the times you saw me start to revel in my pain the way the demons do. I'm sorry for the parts of me that you saw tarnish, not just the ones that broke away from grief but the fragments you saw me chip away myself. I'm sorry for the prayers I distorted into wishes from slices of devils food cake. I'm sorry for all the cuts and bruises that maybe you felt too. That hurt I caught for the sake of chasing away the light thinking I was running after it. I'm sorry the tantalizing voices of those who treated wounds by creating deeper ones caught my ear and not your harmony. I'm sorry for having forsaken myself. I'm sorry I didn't know you to love you. I'm sorry for the girl who lost everything including the sense to not blur right from wrong. I'm sorry for the sins that count against me and maybe you too. I'm sorry I'm the meek human God placed you in charge of. I'm sorry for having torn apart my spirit and dimming your halo. I thank you for the light you gave, the tears you cried with me from heaven, the songs to hush the grief a little ways away, the gifts you helped God depart. I thank you for the patience, the time, and for the dedication it took to not give up on me. I thank you for being my guardian angel when I was the one that's worth less after what sin can toil. Thank you my guardian dear, my angel of God for always staying just like God always has.

I'm sorry to God for the way I turned away. I'm sorry for the falsehoods I thought were better than anyone that could be above the clouds in the skies. I'm hurt by the shame and guilt of what I've done to you father. For having forsaken you before having known you. I'm sorry for the faults I laid at your feet and for the blame I casted on your undeserving shoulders. I was wrong. I was hurting. I was lost. I was sinful. Thank you for your mercy. Thank you for healing me. Thank you for covering me. Thank you for setting me new. Thank you for the doubt. Thank you for the right fear. Thank you for the amassed strength I gained that I can no longer measure. Thank you for the pain that was and now isn't anymore. Thank you for being my father in heaven when I am the one who is undeserving. Thank you for leaving the flock to save this one. To save me. Thank you for my heart restored with cuts and bruises in all its glory. Thank you for the stone my heart no longer remains. Thank you for your hand in saving my soul. Thank you God.

Thank you for the pain. But more so thank you for scars that can be light others follow toward your face like it did for me.

Thank you Papa Bear,
       Thank you Nonna,
              Thank you Mom,

I now have the four pillars within and beyond this world that keeps me steady within my hue of blue and my never ending vast search for more souls to now save.

"Only in eternity shall we see the beauty of the soul, and only then shall we realize what great things were accomplished by interior suffering."

Mother Angelica

Chapter Thirteen
To Venerate My Soul

Iridescence radiated off of the kaleidoscopic shards of glass like pain inflicting overtime through its unbroken serrated truth. Light broke through the hues of myself being seen for the first time in what felt like centuries of the dust, loss, and despair finally lifting and being replaced. Now being restored was incandescence that gleamed blurs of what I knew to be true when I saw him for the first time again, after it all was finished. It was on my birthday. His heart beat my favorite hymn from heaven on earth I'll forever yearn to hear just once. Falling… falling to love and mourn his story. The despair that grows inside my own heart from reading about him. Skin and bones, a vessel of warmth and cold, and the pain of his own pain echoing. Flecks of golden in the mercy he held that wasn't shown to him. Falling back into place. Falling back into myself again. Falling to follow him, I fell into the girl I had always dreamed of through my writing that I'd become. Drawn towards the altar, the candlelight alighting the tragedy and beauty all intertwined together. Looking up to see those dual halos for eyes staring back into mine from above. Falling into my spirit, falling into my grace, falling into my faith. By breath, by healing, by prayer, by dual hearts beating together mine here and his in heaven; catching onto light he sent unto me. I hear God, I feel his presence and I feel whole again. I fell into the hue of blue the holy bible speaks of as peace. I fell into God's arms after I had died in them. He brought me back. I fell holding God's hand this time. Breaking to heal. Isolated but not alone. No longer breaking to heal. Healing to break. By his light that shines through my scars, my ever hindered and bruised body and flesh. By brokenness I was watered, nurtured, cleaned, and I became whole again. It's not about the wounds themselves and who put them there. It's what to do with them. I became God's child again finally. I became a part of his story as he is ever sent a part of mine. I became one with my soul. I became a daughter of light.

The timeless tender call I experienced from Christ;

When God calls you by name, he not only will command you to walk around the darkness. Sometimes when it is called for especially, he will call you to walk through it. And knowing him, garners you to know yourself. Once you know your name and it's truth wears bright, he gives you a new one.

Deanna Marie Battista

So as bright as day I had always been called, God now defers to me as the daughter of light.

Philomena; Deanna Marie Battista

What led me to picking St. Philomena as my confirmation saint? I tell you not just by God's divine timing, but his will alone. The day he called my name, it was this time I had heard it audibly. Years prior through my interior suffering, internal anguish, I mourned and grieved the loss I thought I had shed of purity, grace and virtue because I thought these divitinies had been stolen from me. Along with my lightly covered flecks of innocence. I hadn't realized God was helping me find, through all of this reckoning and crucifying these exact divinites I thought had been taken away. All death's deserve to be mourned but only a few deserve it to be done beautifully intertwined with the pain of that loss. Not just seemingly bringing flowers to your own grave. But learning how to grow and plant new seeds where they will take root wrapped around the light directly from heaven, down and around to the soul of the child he is trying to get back and reawaken. To breathe life back into. This was my experience as well. He had called me tenfold, many times while I couldn't hear, and slowly I started to chip away at the sin and not the ground beneath my feet that I needed to walk upon. I started to ferment in this torment. This is what made me beautiful. God used my pain, and showed me the way. Then came the day he called my name in a voice I could hear. Truly I tell you, the random day at the office alone and surrounded by silence with nothing but my writing of breaking chains and creating this book Ice Cream Sunday to burn ever so brightly as he was leading me to do so. My journey was just getting started however. How humor interjected into the deafening of no noise can bring such startling understanding. God has a sense of humor. Something else I learned on this whirlwind of a heaven sent journey. He called me, and it was the overwhelming feeling of being "seen" that made me immediately think of angels. I eventually laughed at myself for thinking this weeks later. Yes he has definitely sent me angels, this I know. But it was he who called me by my name, "Deanna". He shows us who he is, and we don't see, he tells us who he is and we don't hear. Much like the apostles my comprehension was not coherent. Though, as soon as I went home I called my church and immediately started the process of getting confirmed in my faith. It wasn't something I was avoiding, just something I'd always do in the future. From that day on- I started the process and this is what led me to my saint. To her and even more so myself. This was the faintest of whispers that felt like a letter from heaven. Philomena. Thanks be to God.

Chapter Fourteen
God Showed Me His Heart and Ignited Mine

Luke 1:78 (zecaraiah's prophecy)
"By the tender mercy of our God, the dawn upon us to give light to those who sit in darkness and in the shadow of death to guide our feet into the way of peace."

My faith looked as if it had broken away when I never really had it to begin with. My faith didn't break, but it was my idea of faith that had completely shattered. So the story goes when you know of God instead of knowing God; at least that's how my story went. I looked for him in stunted urgency without realizing it was him I was looking for. And in all the wrong places, even on a miniscule level it can feel like mountains between you and what's right. And that's knowing him, just like it's being known by him. When you knock on enough doors one of them will open but it can close behind you, locking not just you inside, but inside of yourself as well. It takes great strength, will and torment to be able to open that door and find to follow God. It's the spiritual battle most don't realize they asked for. I know I didn't. I reached my hand into the darkness looking for my creator with my face turned away from him at the same time. The allure of what can be found in pain when the darkness whispers out to you, seductive and inviting. Trying to soothe away the doubt and interject the multiple echoes of the gravely fallen. No one had to tell me that the darkness would be dark, but I still wish someone would have. Silly and foolish little girl I was. Changing my ideas of what a foundation of religion looked like. The taking of pain away because we definitely don't deserve to suffer right? Wrong. Suffering is a gift that I hadn't realized, funny because I knew suffering very well. But pain is painful. And the truth hurts. So why gravitate to the faith that not only measures your suffering but also teaches you how to use it. Because pain is something we all try to avoid. Not that little girl, she didn't understand the intricate detail of pain and the beauty of it. She just wanted to not be sick anymore. She just didn't want to feel the finality of the absence Papa left when he left her in this world without him. She just didn't want the entirety of her being eviscerated by a man who couldn't hear her tears. Mercy from suffering was what I was after but suffering mercilessly was what I gained instead. The tarnish of the soul, what a fickle thing. Especially when it is by our own hand, because we all know best right. Not maybe the one who created us, but the created themselves? Looking for my creator but not knowing it was him I was looking for. What a separation of truth, of discernment, and of grace. Looking for him in the statue of buddha, in the lotus flower and passing by the doubt the confusion of it all brought on. Looking for life, when I felt like a shadow away from death. And so my journey continued through the dark forest of my internal suffering, following the crumbs but not of bread. In the darkness I went like a simulation of a little "blue" riding hood. Then came the blunt force trauma of my ignorance, looking for God but listening to the devil. " The devil knows your name, but calls us by our sins. God knows our sins, but calls us by our name." I have experienced both. In the rabbit hole I sought out welcoming the "healing", the poison that is the forbidden fruit of the world, on the inside once you take a bite. I took more than one. One should have been more than enough. In my haste to be pain-free I faltered and thus began the realest suffering I have experienced to date. So the witchcraft books and the tarot cards, astrology and new world age blasphemy wrapped in a ribbon of more bitter and less sweet ungodliness roared. This ribbon I then choose to tie my eyes blind with. Then calling out to the depths of the wicked; I do confess. Looking for God by playing advocate to the devil. Naive little girl I had been, because the darkness clung to me, but I initiated that discretion to parts of my soul I thought I didn't want by grasping desperately of the darkness first. God took note of the entirety of that naive little girl's innocent suffering, the insidiousness of my pain inflicted by others, and the gift my suffering was I had missed. This led me to strike my own hand to snuff out the light I wanted to be but didn't know how to become. How does one become light in nothing but darkness? That's what I was really after.

So when he pricked my conscience and the doubt spread the fear like nothing I had ever held before, it broke through every wound and scar I had both healed and unhealed. The whole time through my crucifying he was there and I stopped looking and learned to see him. There was this mercilessness that did in fact have mercy within it. The more I suffered in this spiritual battle for myself back, the more the light shone through and the darkness began to slip away. I entered into a state of complete and total anguish. But God showed me the beauty of it. He showed me the beauty of my pain, then taught me how to use it. To carry my cross no matter how many times I fell, I got back up and learned to use it for others more so. After the fall I had to grace, he healed me even though I didn't pray for him too. I now try to measure the gifts he's given me and gift them to others.

As I mentioned I had taken more than one bite of the forbidden when I should have known better. Thank God my suffering preserved me because after the insidiousness that had happened, it made me question and rethink everything compared to before my trust was completely broken. Not just with that person who had broken it, but within myself, within my idea of faith and also within my entire purview of how I viewed the world's take on love, romance, and men. Trying to correlate it back to the little girl I had used to be, even though I still was, I became a shell of her. I was trying to correlate it back to the girl who used to look for prince charming and dream about fairytales. After I was shredded through the reckoning I didn't know would be a version of a death of me. I became very defiant and rebellious within my bubble that I constructed myself over the years out of fear, that eventually became my cell. But I "needed" it. Even in my innocent and naive manner. I was trying to eviscerate and destroy my innocence and purity in the bits and pieces that he had missed and left behind for me to die over and over again by. I seeked out lust not knowing what I'd find, but hoping I would achieve. For me it was about desecrating my innocence and destroying my purity because that is what he had done to me. Because the pieces that floated around in my heart and mind that were untainted, I just couldn't take the good they were, when I wasn't anymore. I couldn't take what was left of the lamb when I was covered in the filth of assault. So I wanted to snuff them out. The way he had me. The never ending cycle of abuse sometimes can turn around tenfold and that's when I raised my own hand. So always being in my bubble and alone, never going past the end of my driveway left me with the four walls of my bedroom to reflect back like mirrors with nothing but my suffering to hold in my hands this time. Aside from the books and the allure of twisting pain into more pain without realizing it. There was one tiny window that alighted in the darkness but can be anything but. The internet. It was about breaking apart the girl that would have wished upon a star for the prince in Cinderella to come and save her, because in the very back end of this ridiculous man-hating false empowered promiscuity, and unheavenly outlook which I'm happy I never took to face value. Though this is true, still there were some slight similarities to the ground I started to chip away at that Papa had spent years pouring the foundation of what a man is supposed to be. His death and what happened after erased parts of his hard work, and that made me want to die all over again. The hues in what the darkness distorted around and within my way of convincing myself this is okay, this is normal, this isn't fear, or pain and confusion or curiosity all mixed together. It was just another way to blot out this light that I was searching for and losing at the same time. By trying to find through the map the devil lies before us to distract away from the footsteps that are always near to follow Christ. I am lucky even within what felt like endless suffering. I faltered, and fell but I did not lose my soul. I may have bruised it along the way but I am thankful I had God call me by name away from the dismay my mind started to convince me was real, and not sin and more so not a spiritual death when that's exactly what it was. God pricked my conscience while the devil pierced through my virtue. My virtue, I didn't lose it though I mourned and grieved like I had. God heard my yearn, and I heard his voice. The rest is (his)tory.

    I was the carpenter of my own pain splintered by the cross I carried at my own will of loathing light while seeking darkness, thinking the darkness I could hold would illuminate my pain and pierce through the light of my daunting days. While Jesus was nailed to the cross at the will of his love for us. I ignored every warning and washed my hands in the dirt trying to get them as clean as snow. The never ending heartbreak that led to heaven and I weeping together. Then and forever now, but the tears that ring out today are as beautiful as thorns and as enduring as steel.

    The moon shines light in total darkness. I just wanted a piece of that to keep with me, especially if I couldn't refine myself in sorrow enough to become something that resembled a silver flame. I felt like my reflection became a starless sky. I just wanted to reignite from every flicker that had gone out in my eyes. I wanted to bring light to darkness, because that is the true reason even if we don't know it, some of us dwell there. I didn't know God does that too. That is why the darkness is not dark to him at all, and now I no longer fear the dark. Now I can command it. Because God showed me his heart and ignited mine. Because now we both carry something sacred inside.

Chapter Fifteen
The End Is Just the Start

Finding my way through the darkness was something I had to learn at a very young age, as most do in this life. But specifically walking on sinful colored glass through a version of darkness to find God. That was something that took all of me with it, and broke the parts of me along that way that it was meant to. Years passed after finding him, fermenting in my faith enough to really learn, appreciate, and share in his great works and the miracle I even became by his own hand and maybe a little of mine too. The overwhelming peace he has given me. I want to give back.

To have met with the darkness in a naive vacate choice was a humorless decision of foolishness. I had made out of ignorance and out of the childish misguided confusion and allure of who God was and who the devil wasn't. What a shadow of doubt that could lead someone so astray like it did me. When time healed all things through the mercy and glory of God, I began a vocation I like to call my little portion before I walk through the vocation of marriage and motherhood. Though all of the halls of my pain I will keep with me close. Not in a box of hurt, but in an array of published works; of the pieces that I both found and lost that I hope my future children can learn from one day. Through the vocation of pain, and now of spreading his word. I pray one day to begin the truest form of love I can find never aside but right next to loving Christ. Being a Mommy! So here I began writing this story, the trials, the pain, the loss, laughter, and the agony of what life and death can pose. Losing Papa to cancer. Losing myself to sexual assault and harassment. Thinking of a boy in a bright royal blue sweatshirt that adorned the halls of highschool with wings from heaven that might have actually been a real life angel. To the cuts and bruises that my childishness caught. I wouldn't have changed one beautiful gift or terror filled curse. I survived and I created this book not only as a testament to that, but so others can use it to lay their experiences within it too. Learn from me, you who are reading this. Love God the way I wish I always would have. The truest takeaway, I want this book to reflect, that my kindness is not weakness. Why should I believe others when they tell me so? Not everyone has a fist that can punch through steel. Some have the ability of forgiveness to cut through sin instead. So to the fight of a girl whose faith, grace and femininity became her sword, her scars and pain became her shield and the word of God in tune with her heart and mind became the greatest defense she's ever known… armor. I'm proud of you. You've endured so much in this life, I can only imagine what could be waiting in the next. The delicacy in how she doesn't have to carry weapons to win the battle but, know God to know herself to win the war. I'm proud of every fragment both broken and healed you've become.

- Your older self.

And to all the readers, and my family who read this book. Thank you for enduring the pain I went through to learn from it. Like I said in the beginning, don't carry my death, I don't anymore. Carry my message. Because I promise you, it's truly worth more.

- Deanna Marie.

*"O Lord, everything good in me is due to you.
The rest is my fault."*

St. Augustine

Outro

Forgive me father for I have sinned, I was old enough to know right from wrong, but yet I did not understand the insidiousness of what that man was doing enough for me to scream out and not inwardly take accountability for what was not my doing. Yet I felt the insidiousness and understood that's what it was. I've forsaken myself many times over the years because of this. No more. I can't blame the man even tempted by the devil, he was just a man. I have forgiven him. But myself, that was who I was struggling with forgiving the most. Because even though I was just a girl, I raised my hand and did everything to desecrate what he yet hadn't. Even tempted by the devil I was just a girl. I have forgiven her. I know now it wasn't my fault. The armor of God I have inherited by my pain and torment. Yet truth is what I will always strive to seek no matter how much it stings, because I know what happens when you lack it. I delfied my purity just for the sake of doing it in hopes it would erase my hurt completely. I confess father, please rid me of the insidiousness I then turned onto myself and committed against her, without knowing you. I'm sorry. For my gravest sins led me to the grave, you called out to me without audible echo first yet my soul and the bones in my body felt that earth shaking noise. You came for me, and I now follow you. Not half heartedly and not with shame of myself anymore. Look upon my face, please father. Not because I want to further punish myself, it is not about owning my sins, but not letting my sins own me. Look upon my face because I do not want to hide from you anymore. I want you to see me, not that you haven't always. I want to acknowledge that power that I found in the gifts and graces you have given me. I earned them though I don't feel like I have. Forgive me father for I have sinned.

Bare it all in this life so you can inherit it all in heaven.
-Deanna Marie Battista

Final Word

The name you all take away from this book is not my own. It's Jesus Christ. He's the one who saved me; I'm just the girl he saved. Nothing more and nothing less. I'm just Deanna Marie. The credit and glory belong to him, now and always.

Luke 15:7

"Just so, I tell you, there will be more joy in heaven over one sinner who repents than over ninety-nine righteous people who need no repentance."

In Loving Memory of

Ulisse Battista
February 18th, 1944 - December 19th, 2013

Thank you Papa for the times you've traveled with my heart from this earth to heaven. For the times you wiped my tears away and kept me from falling. For the strength and butterfly wings you left. For the promise your presence became even though we are so far apart. Thank you for holding my hand even when I let go. Thank you for the pain you helped wash away that stung from you leaving me. Thank you for helping me find my voice when I could no longer hear yours. For the brightest gift you allowed me to hold, thank you for the light I now write with Papa, because of me, because of you. Thank you for being my angel on the moon. Until we dance and sing again, in the sky where the stars that once burned out now shine like we do. I'll carry you with me, not your death but our story.

About The Author

Deanna Marie Battista is 24 years old and lives in Upstate New York with her parents and little beagle Buddy Balboa. When she is not writing or reading she is working on her two small businesses; bella luna crystal's boutique, and the fairy house. She loves going to craft fairs and bringing her creations to life as well as sharing her love for God to others. She also teaches bible study on youtube, Sunday-Brunchwithdeannamarie and loves attending mass as much as possible to share God's word. Deanna just recently started a blog called Letters From Heaven where she has her online portfolio, any of her upcoming projects will be announced there. Follow Deanna Marie on her socials to stay updated on when her next book will be launching. Deanna's next book titled The moon in her is breaking is coming very soon.

Stay connected with Deanna Marie to keep up with all her upcoming projects and new book releases!

www.lettersfromheavenblog.com

◉ @deannamariebattista

▶ www.youtube.com/@sundaybrunchwithdeannamarie

Become apart of the journey like all the other angels, fairies, bluebells, and blue ribbons to adhere to the road we will all walk and face together answering God's call while heeding his message as Deanna does;

always writing with light

Isaiah 44:22

"I have swept away your transgressions like a cloud, and your sins like mist; return to me, for I have redeemed you."